LOOPHOLE

An anthology of Criminal Cases

Clyde S. Munsell

Attorney at Law

Clyde S. Munsell
Chula Vista, CA 91910
Clydemunsell@gmail.com

This novel is a work of non-fiction. Only the names of characters have been changed to protect their identities.

Library of Congress Cataloging in Publication
Munsell, Clyde S.
Loophole
Printed in the United States
Loophole/by Clyde S. Munsell

NON-FICTION/LEGAL
ISBN 10: 1497524555
ISBN 13: 978-1497524552

Cover & Interior design by Ron Sharrow
Author photo by Andrew Munsell

Table of Contents

To Loring

Prologue

*"It is better that ten guilty persons
escape than one innocent suffer."*
William Blackstone, 1765

Introduction

have been a criminal defense attorney for more than 42 years. While the last 32 of those years were marked by crystal sobriety, the first decade was draped in drunken drudgery.

Largely because I was originally disdainful and somewhat incapable of afternoon court appearances, I began to explore a method of avoiding them, including trials. Of necessity, I developed a system of achieving successful dispositions of criminal cases through negotiation. The results were achieved by default rather than by decision. This process eventually resulted in freedom for my clients in 99% of the cases. In retrospect, my methods proved successful in the more than 3,000 felony cases I handled.

With sobering clarity of mind, I perfected a methodology whereby I generally knew the eventual outcome of each case at the outset of my representation.

Although I tried to teach this simple approach to more than three dozen transient associates in my law office, not one of them could comprehend these simple tools of practice. Even though I tutored them in the permutations of my pursuits, they continued to remain bewildered by the technique. I continued to observe absolute disbelief of the results predicted by the empirical evidence, even though they were active participants in a successful team effort.

The reader may glean some insight into these fact-based stories, each different but essentially the same…all resulting in the freedom of the defendant…even the otherwise undeserving.

Clyde Munsell

I

Black and Blue

The gun misfired the second time Bessie pulled the trigger. Otherwise, she probably would have killed her live-in boyfriend, a Navy bluejacket. When the cops showed up and arrested her, there were still five bullets left in the .38 caliber revolver. The first of the six shots did not misfire; it was buried deep in the belly of her lover. He had been holding her captive in their apartment and using her for a punching bag for a day and a half. When she had enough, she grabbed his Saturday-night-special and shot him.

One of her friends knew Clyde and asked him to visit Bessie at the women's jail. There he found a small, young, beaten and bruised black woman. She was in a blue funk, depressed, despondent and with an attitude of fatalistic futility. Clyde listened to her story and warned her that she needed to tell him the whole story…to leave nothing out. She agreed to tell Clyde the whole story.

Bessie was unemployed and virtually destitute. She had a small personal injury award pending which would be barely enough to cover the expenses of her defense. Clyde agreed to accept an assignment of the proceeds when the personal injury case was settled and represent her for the payment of costs with no promise of a fee.

When Clyde met with the prosecutor to discuss a settlement of the charges against her, he learned that Bessie had told him virtually nothing about her situation. The Assistant District Attorney informed him that this incident was the third boyfriend Bessie had maimed and nearly killed. Each prior incident was similar, having involved a period of confinement and battering. In the first incident, she bit the eyelid off of her *lover* and in the second, she stabbed her boyfriend in the head with a butcher knife. There was a pattern to Bessie's love life and her selection of companions. The prosecutor was determined to make the latest incident her final violent assault, before she succeeded in killing someone.

Clyde believed that incarceration without treatment and rehabilitation would not end her compulsion for abuse and murderous revenge. She would be locked away and eventually released from prison with no resolution of her psychological problems and in all likelihood seek a relationship with a new abuser and repeat the cycle. However, he was keenly aware that the criminal justice system offered few if any opportunities for the kind of treatment she needed, particularly for black women who were considered by the system to be disposable.

He engineered a plan to get her the treatment she needed and keep her out of prison, so her three little children would not be placed in the welfare-operated foster-care system. His first step was to locate the right psychologist to conduct an evaluation. He found a black, lesbian, women's rights activist who was willing to undertake the task of examining Bessie. She reported that she was mentally afflicted and in need of medical supervision, not imprisonment.

With the report in hand, Clyde presented it to a young, extremely liberal, eager-beaver County welfare system psychologist to elicit a second opinion. Anxious to please and unwilling to refute the first report, her report enthusiastically affirmed the conclusion of the earlier report.

Not satisfied with the two opinions of psychologists whose credentials might be challenged by the prosecutor, he wanted a third report from a clinical psychologist in private practice with more experience. He agreed to pay her a small fee for her services. After studying the two prior reports, the private psychologist closed ranks with her colleagues and produced an unequivocal affirmation of those opinions in a third report.

Armed with three consistent reports, Clyde plotted to eliminate the chance of the prosecutor refuting his psychologists' opinions. He sought yet another opinion from the eminent psychologist who regularly acted as the District Attorney's expert witness. This resulted in a fourth report which was in authoritative solidarity with the other three reports. Now, the District Attorney's favorite expert witness had a conflict of interest and would be unable to testify for the prosecution.

The first procedural step in the system was the preliminary hearing, followed by the readiness conference. Finally, there was the settlement conference, the last step before trial. To Clyde's dismay, the matter was set before Judge Harrington, the strictest, toughest, most cantankerous judge on the local bench.

It was just before Christmas. Clyde had Bessie's children, ages two, three and five, come to court dressed in new, white, Sunday-go-to-meetin' outfits. This was an unorthodox practice in those days. When Clyde identified the three shining little angels to the judge as the defendant's children, the old crank became irate, probably because he was also unavoidably moved and didn't want it to show.

The Judge berated Clyde and advised that bringing children into the courtroom was inappropriate. Clyde assured the judge that he was totally embarrassed by having inadvertently transgressed and being unaware of any rule that prohibited his conduct. He pledged that he would never do such a thing again. Shortly after that incident, signs were posted on the doors of all of the criminal courtrooms announcing, **NO ONE UNDER 18 ADMITTED.**

The settlement conference was set for one month later before the same judge. With the four psychologists' reports including that of the District Attorney's favorite expert, the

3

prosecution was unable to find anyone with the credentials to contradict the reported clinical findings.

The reports established that Bessie was a lifelong victim of abuse, whose personality disorder was at the root of her victimization. Her repetitive masochism and subsequent violent outbursts were pre-structured, virtually unavoidable and beyond her control. She required professional treatment which could not be successfully provided while confined in a penal institution. The reports recommended that she be placed on probation contingent upon her receiving the needed treatment.

The judge did not fail to note when rendering his judgment that Clyde had single-handedly upset the entire criminal justice system. He indicated that he had no choice but to follow the recommendations of the defendant's experts. Despite her two prior convictions for violent felonies, he reluctantly granted her probation and Bessie walked free to return to her children and seek the medical attention she so desperately needed.

Though Bessie never realized it, her personal suffering became the inspiration for hope, and the refuge of a multitude of similarly victimized women. Her case became the clinical linchpin and legal bulwark, not only in California, but across the nation, for the *Battered Woman Syndrome* defense. It led to the advancement of humane principles becoming requisite in the administration of justice.

2
A Tall Man's Tale

t is difficult for a seven-foot-tall white man accompanied by his six-foot-eight girlfriend not to stand out in a crowd. So it is quite amazing that Harry Kraft escaped detection and remained a fugitive from federal justice for seven years.

The caliber of his criminal escapades were of such gigantic proportions, that in the early frontier days, Harry would have achieved a level of fame that would have equaled Jesse James or Butch Cassidy and the Sundance Kid.

He conducted his drug dealing business in the style of a swashbuckling adventurer. He chartered a plane in Los Angeles with a flight plan for a roundtrip to Houston and back. Once in the air, he forced the pilot to fly to Mexico and land on a beach, where his waiting compadres stuffed the aircraft full of marijuana. The plane crashed and burned because it was too heavy to take off. Harry and the pilot got out unhurt and Harry got away. The pilot reported him for kidnapping, air piracy and attempting smuggling. For more than seven years, Harry had his portrait on display on post office walls all over the United States.

Meanwhile, south of the border, one of Harry's main amigos got slammed into the hoosegow, so Harry engineered his escape. He hired a hard-core drug-running helicopter pilot and had everything timed so that when they landed in the prison exercise yard, his convict friend could quickly jump aboard. Unfortunately, one of the prison guards got onto the whirlybird's landing strut, where he was shot and killed by the otherwise ineffective gunfire of the other guards. The helicopter flew off into the clouds to become legend when this caper became the basis for the Charles Bronson film, *Breakout*.

As it turned out, Harry was not arrested for his participation in that gambol. He and his Amazon girlfriend were swept up in the takedown of a huge cocaine conspiracy. The conspiracy was so gigantic that just to fund it, they had established an enormous marijuana enterprise, so extensive they had their own private airport in Arizona. In addition to the staff pilots, there were maintenance, farming, distribution and administrative personnel. In all, 36 culprits were involved, including four lawyers.

Clyde was retained to represent Harry for the defense of the criminal case against him. The wife of Harry's principal co-conspirator came to his office with a plush, blue velveteen presentation bag for Royal Crown whiskey filled with $10,000.00 in cash. The stated purpose of the bag full of money was that it was intended to be given to a *bagman* to bribe away Harry's legal problems.

Clyde applied the money to his fee and informed the U.S. Attorney that he had been retained by a third party. He then set about sequestering Harry's property and securing it in a storage facility before it could be searched and impounded. The Feds had already seized $12,000.00 Harry had hidden in his socks when he was nabbed.

Harry was indicted on 113 counts, the penalties for which totaled life imprisonment plus 115 years. Clyde knew that a case of this size and complexity would take more than a year to get to trial and would be a costly administrative nightmare for the prosecution. A plea bargain arrangement was the obvious method of resolving the case. Clyde's challenge was to insure his client got the benefit of such a bargain.

He began contacting counsel for the other defendants to get their opinions of a possible settlement. They all recognized that their clients had great exposure, especially since some of the defendants, who were themselves attorneys, would be looking to sell out their co-conspirators to save their own licenses, careers and carcasses.

As the case unfolded, the original co-defendants who were attorneys were not the only lawyers who would create problems. During the case, the legal representatives for four defendants were themselves arrested and indicted for other unrelated criminal matters. While their clients were unrepresented, settlement negotiations and progress in the case became stalled and came to a screeching halt. This situation created problems for the prosecution as well as for the attorneys of the other defendants. But as often is the case, one man's problems can be another's opportunities.

In the Federal system a lawyer can represent only one client in any criminal case, so Clyde could not directly undertake the representation of the defendants whose lawyers had been busted. He arranged for four of his pals who were lawyers to enter their appearances on behalf of the four unrepresented defendants. They were essentially empty suits who would be front-men to go along with Clyde's plans. By keeping the case moving and avoiding delays, he was able to help all of the defendants and their lawyers. More important, he benefited his client because he gained considerable clout in the plea bargaining by controlling the negotiations for five defendants instead of just one.

Clyde was negotiating with Assistant U.S. Attorney, Ed Dorsey, with whom he had never had any previous dealings. Ed was a stylish, younger fellow who Clyde had learned was single, but wasn't quite sure of his sexual orientation. Either way, Clyde wanted to create the impression that he was on Ed's side, so he let his hair grow and began wearing wire-rim glasses and three piece suits, just like Ed. Ed seemed to appreciate that Clyde was helping to keep the case moving by coordinating his efforts with the lawyers for the other defendants. Eventually he and Clyde made a deal. They agreed that each of the defendants would get sentences of ten years or less and Clyde's client would be sentenced to only four years.

At the sentencing hearing the sentences were imposed as agreed, but when it came to Harry Kraft, Ed Dorsey reneged on the agreement. He turned backstabber and argued for a sentence of ten years instead of the agreed upon term of only four years. Maybe he didn't like Clyde's look after all.

The judge was a former defense attorney turncoat who always bent over backward, or maybe forward, to prove his new alliance with the system by caving in to the prosecution's position. So he sentenced Harry Kraft to ten years. He was technically correct because it was within the parameters of the plea bargain, even though it was not in accordance with the verbal agreement between Clyde and Ed Dorsey.

At the conclusion of the hearing, Harry Kraft rose to his full seven-feet, raised his arm its full length toward the bench and flipped off the judge. When he was removed from the courtroom to the holding sell, he stuffed enough paper down the toilet to completely stop it up, flooding the clerk's office and courtroom, and ruining the carpet in the judge's chambers.

The vandalism and intentional destruction of property added to Clyde's troubles, but was not the biggest problem. The main problem was that he could not legally impugn the prosecutor's conduct just because he didn't keep his word. Although it is a tossup, there is usually more honor among lawyers than among thieves. The ancient code of the professional wheeler-dealers is a step above ethics and courtesy; reliance upon your adversary's word permits the flexibility to facilitate quick results, without having to negotiate the cumbersome impediments of rigid judicial rules and regulations that litter the route to the final destination. It works because it is informal, but when it fails, there is no formal remedy.

It galled Clyde that his only recourse was to ask Ed to honor his agreed upon recommendation. In a caustic and condescending response, Ed advised Clyde that he was free to file a Rule 35 Motion to Modify the Sentence, which was his client's absolute right under the law anyway. Clyde did file, but Ed still refused to acknowledge his prior commitment to recommend a four-year sentence to extract a guilty plea. As a result the Court granted a one-year reduction; Harry was facing nine years of incarceration instead of ten, more than twice the time the parties had agreed to.

In Clyde's mind this was an aggravated insult that required an aggressive response. Dorsey's supervisor was Sam Oswald, one of Clyde's longtime friendly adversaries in the U.S. Attorney's office. Clyde met with him to discuss the problem he was having with Ed Dorsey. Sam did not seem surprised by Clyde's revelation. Clyde came away with the distinct impression that this was not the first controversy involving Ed Dorsey. Sam could not intervene to reverse what happened in the courtroom...that was a done deal, unprincipled prosecutor notwithstanding.

Without committing himself, Sam implied that Clyde should do whatever he felt was appropriate to correct the situation and Sam would do what he could to help. The 120-day window for filing Rule 35 motions was still open; Clyde filed another motion, this time bifurcating the issues. By doing this he kept the sentence modification process open. Since the moving party could control the timing of the hearing, Clyde was able to delay the prosecution-pandering judge from ruling on any of the issues until Clyde was prepared.

The key issue in the plea negotiation was that Harry would plead to a count in the cocaine conspiracy, but there was no cocaine involved and none introduced into evidence. Under the Federal parole guidelines then in effect, the actual time a defendant would have to serve was determined by the amount of cocaine involved in the case. The mandatory time to be served had little to do with time ordered in the sentence under the guidelines in effect before November, 1988. Since there was no cocaine in evidence, Harry's mandatory time behind bars could not be determined.

By keeping the Rule 35 Motion to Modify process open and held in abeyance, Clyde was able to schedule a parole hearing before the judge would have an opportunity to rule on the sentence modification. The parole hearing, which was not subject to appeal or modification, established with finality that no cocaine was involved, thereby removing the issue from consideration during the Rule 35 hearing. The judge could still rule favorably on the bargained and agreed to four-year sentence.

Clyde's surprise attack further besmirched Ed Dorsey's reputation. In addition to his supervisor's awareness of his venal dealings with Clyde, his perfidious character and, no doubt, other instances of unprincipled conduct must have been accumulating in his record. Ed Dorsey was dismissed from the U.S. Attorney's office. With Ed's disappearance, the case was reassigned to Sam Oswald.

Since Clyde had established that no cocaine was involved in the case, Sam did not oppose the originally bargained for sentence of four years. At that time, one-third of the sentence was automatically abated in the Federal system. As a result, Harry Kraft walked out tall and free after serving only three years, three months, three weeks and three days behind bars.

Not surprisingly, a short time after his release, Harry's outlaw mentality and habits re-emerged and he reverted to the owl-hoot trail. He was prosecuted for violation of his parole and returned to prison. Clyde did not have the opportunity to defend him the second time. Maybe justice prevailed after all.

3
Bust Out

As a young man, Gustavo (Gus) Heinrich led an idyllic life as a member of the rich, elite in Argentina. Even though the family was Jewish, they were among the privileged few. His father owned the largest newspaper in Buenos Aires and had unfettered access to the ruling regime and the amenities accorded their minions.

Their privileged life, however, took a sudden turn when Juan Peron died and Eva fled from Argentina. Overnight, the void created a vortex into which the warring political parties were sucked in a deadly and unprincipled grab for power. As a Peronist by belief and political choice, Gus's father fell prey to the Junta. He was toppled from his pedestal and stripped of his wealth. The new military government was desperately short of funds and made it clear that it intended to use all means within its power, including non-judicial means to further its goals.

Gus, an attorney, was in New York City studying for a master's degree in his chosen field of immigration and extradition laws at New York University. He received word that the family was in trouble and returned home. His homecoming was welcomed by utter chaos and the unbelievable atrocities which were occurring on a daily basis.

He was approached by members of an opposition military Junta who demanded that he participate in a massive fraud scheme when he returned to America. They knew that Gus had worked as an attorney in immigration and extradition cases, but had also been a member of the travel bureau agencies in the United States. The Junta was not discouraged by his refusal to use his legal skills and experience in the travel industry to further their political interests. Within two weeks, Gus's eighteen-month old nephew was kidnapped, taken to a town square, publicly thrown into the air and skewered on the end of a soldier's bayonet. Gus went into hiding with the surviving members of his family.

Not to be denied, the Junta hunted down and murdered his mother and his fiancé in La Plata. Gus's name was scrawled in their blood on a public wall as evidence tying him to the murders. Beaten, Gus contacted the chief general of the pre-Alfonse regime to make a deal to save the rest of his family and himself. They agreed to ignore the murder charges against him if he would assist them with their fraud scheme in the United States. In addition, they were to pay him $100,000.00 for his efforts. The money would be paid to the general who would arrange for the dismissal of the murder charges. Having no options, Gus agreed.

His role was to mount and mastermind a massive fraud of the travel agencies and major airlines in the United States. Gus returned to the United States and began contacting and organizing the expatriate groups of Argentineans to put together the scheme. To his surprise, he found among the 300 members of the operation, Peronists, members of the ruling military Junta and a group loyal to a third opposition political party.

The coup against President Isabel Peron was in March, 1976. The military Junta that overthrew the government ruled until October, 1983 and was involved in the 1982 Falkland Island war with Great Britain during their rule. The purpose of the scheme engineered by Gus was to raise funds for the several parties vying for power. Although they were involved in a cooperative effort in America, they would end up shooting at each other in Argentina.

Gus infiltrated the primary agencies for the airlines associations and learned there were no audit procedures in place to control the ticket stock supplied to the various travel agencies. Using the services of the New York law firm of Leonard Harrison, Gus created a veil of protection and assistance in developing his plan.

He segregated his 300 members into several groups, in the first of which he played a role. They would prey upon travel agencies across the country that were advertised for sale. They readily agreed to the asking price and the down payment would be made, usually in cash. After the negotiations were concluded, a second group would move in during the first week of operation. Their purpose was to rape the travel agency of the issued but un-audited ticket stock, validate the tickets and sell them on the black-market at cut-rate prices in New York, Los Angeles and Florida.

Among the maneuvers Gus employed was to put a mole in the government agency that approved the sale of travel agencies. When one of the targets of the scam wrote for confirmation to allow their business to be sold to the members of Gus's organization, the mail which was intercepted, received a positive response. Having received approval and the necessary paper work, the sellers of the travel agencies believed they had the blessings of the operative agencies of the United States Government. By the time they failed to receive the second payment on their notes, the bust out was complete, the tickets were gone and the business had been abandoned.

The arrangement worked well for several years. In virtually every large city Gus traveled, detection was impossible. The scheme operated perfectly without problems. As a big city crime, little if anything was done to conduct personal audits of the purchasers prior to the sales at these seemingly wondrous offers of the full asking price with a substantial cash down payment.

The group faltered, however, when they assumed it would be easy to prey upon agencies in small towns. The mistake occurred in Missoula, Montana. Between the time of the first contact and the scheduled closing of the sale, the agency owner attempted to check out Gus's bank references. No one had ever heard of Gus, and the bank references failed to check out. Despite

13

the $13,000.00 down payment, the owner of the travel agency contacted the FBI. They placed agents inside the agency at the time of the closing. Mr. Heinrich was arrested.

A low bail was set in the amount of only $10,000.00, but the group had failed to provide funds for a bond or other exigencies in the event any of its members were apprehended. Gus was stuck. It didn't take long for the FBI to unravel the scheme and tie it to the bust outs that had been occurring nationally over the preceding three years. Bond was raised to $500,000.00 and Gus was moved to the Southern District of California. There, prosecutor Laury Rogers of the U.S. Attorney's office instigated an investigation and unraveled Gus's participation in the national scam.

Ed Cummings referred the defense to Clyde Munsell. Clyde was paid him just enough money to warrant his entering a general appearance in the case. Clyde solicited the help of attorney Charles McCutcheon to review the case and attempt to understand his client's involvement. During their first interview with Gus, they found him to be cagey but cooperative. He explained some of the details of the operation, but it was evident that he was going to say no more than he felt might be required to bring his counsel up to speed.

Within a short period of time, indictments and complaints were issued in San Francisco, Chicago, New York, Missoula and San Diego. The chances of winning in five different Federal Districts were near impossible. In trips to Chicago and Missoula, Clyde learned just how seriously the Feds were taking Gus's activities. Despite the fact that Gus was an attorney, he was labeled as a foreign terrorist. Sentences for others in similar circumstances in Chicago and New York were 50 and 55 years respectively.

In extensive discussions with Ms. Rogers and Judge Janet Keene in the U.S. District court in San Diego, an arrangement was made for Gus to cooperate with the government. In reality, Gus did not intend to cooperate at all, but he was able to buy himself a one-year residence at the New York Metropolitan Correctional Center, while postal authorities interviewed him at their leisure to determine if they could pursue any of the other 300 members of the cabal.

Gus did a masterful job. He never gave up quite enough information to result in anyone else being charged, but he finagled credit for his efforts, achieving the epitome of success for his efforts which led the government down a dead-end street. Upon Gus's return to San Diego, Clyde filed a ream of compelling motions which resulted in all of the counts in the other districts being dismissed or merged into the five counts of mail fraud in the San Diego indictment. Gus pled to those counts before Judge Keene in 1983. During his sentencing, Judge Keene commented that Gus had been involved in the fraud as long as she had been on the bench. By employing a carefully considered tactic of not negotiating with the prosecutor over her determination to commit Gus to the maximum term of six years, Clyde was able to gain a recess of the proceedings for three weeks to prepare all of the affidavits.

Ms. Rogers was upset by the delay, but it was too late for her to do anything about it...she had already committed the Government's position on the record. Clyde had carefully calculated the length of the sentence to coincide with the term of the newly installed ruling Junta. If Gus's extradition proceedings occurred too soon, Gus would have been killed upon his return to Argentina, his previous agreement with the Junta notwithstanding. Even the FBI Agent assigned to the case agreed that Gus would be killed without regard to the fact that he wasn't involved in the double homicide of which he was accused. A lie detector administered at the time absolved him of the homicides, but found that he was guilty of the 300 million dollar mail fraud bust outs.

In the midst of this, the Red Brigade, an Italian terrorist group, kidnapped General James Dozier, the highest ranking military officer in Europe. As luck would have, Clyde had volunteered to introduce the eldest son of a senior member of the United States House of Representatives into a twelve-step program designed to lead to his sobriety. Clyde and the Congressman spoke on a daily basis.

Through his connections, Gus learned of the kidnapping before it had become public knowledge. To further enhance his cooperative efforts, he told Clyde that he could locate the general...even from his jail cell in California. In short order, he provided Clyde with specific information about where the general was being held captive.

The Congressman put Clyde in contact with the Office to Combat Terrorism in Washington, D.C. Clyde conveyed the information he had received from Gus, namely, that General Dozier was being held in a room over a bakery in Padua, Italy.

Two week later the U.S. Government announced that they found and rescued the General at the exact location provided by Gus. Clyde's assistance was never acknowledged and the Office to Combat Terrorism never returned any of Clyde's calls.

Besides General Dozier, the only person who benefited from the information that led to his rescue was Gus, who received a substantial reduction in his sentence. At least now, General Dozier, knows who was responsible for saving his life.

Gus was sentenced to a six-year term, which would actually only require that he serve four years. His release from custody would occur right after the military Junta was out of power. Extradition proceedings began immediately. Clyde had never been paid for his services beyond the amount of the original small retainer. An attorney was appointed to handle the extradition proceedings.

By the time the case got to the Supreme Court where it was lost, Gus's concern about being executed was over. The military Junta was out of power and President Alfonsin was in power, busily engaged in the investigation of the disappearance of more than 6000 Argentineans.

By then, Gus had become thoroughly entrenched in a life of crime. He was involved in a $180,000.00 extortion attempt from a fellow inmate, for which he was pursued until the time he boarded the plane for his return to Argentina. He received only a five-month suspended sentence for his efforts, the judge noting that it hardly mattered, since he was being deported anyway.

After having exhausted his remedies at the Supreme Court, he was returned to Argentina where he faced a trial on the homicide charges. While other matters kept him in custody, the homicide charges were not provable for a number of reasons, the least of which was that the wall upon which his name had been painted with the victims' blood had been over painted with house paint prior to any photographs or chemical test having been taken.

When the Peronists regained power, President Carlos Mehem granted Gus a pardon. Gus, in a never ending series of international intrigues, had dug himself into a hole so deep he could never hope to extricate himself. His fortune and privilege had been lost and his life had become indelibly colored into one of ever evolving crime.

In 1988, Clyde received a letter from Gus thanking him for his representation and acknowledging his indebtedness of the *large* fees he owed. Clyde has not heard from him since.

4
No Time for Clocking

im Hewitt had always been in the used car business, one way or another. He was also a long-time member of Alcoholics Anonymous. Overcoming years of ups and downs, he settled into a serene life of sobriety and eked out a modest living as an independent dealer. He didn't have a car lot…just a simple office on the fringe of the downtown area. He diligently investigated the multitude of private sales advertised in the newspapers, buying the few low-mileage, well-kept, reliable models and reselling these cherries to his numerous friends and acquaintances. He was well known in the A.A. community as the man to see when you were sober enough to drive again.

Jake North was not a member of A.A…he was just a local used-car dealer who had cultivated a relationship with an upstate big-city auto auction. He knew Jim Hewitt by reputation as someone who worked the private sale market. He arranged with Jim to scout the market for the kind of vehicles which were of particular interest to him.

Jake was interested in good-looking, quality cars, but they didn't have to be the low-mileage gems like the vehicles Jim selected for his own clientele. The mileage was of no consequence to Jake, because his son was a mechanic with expertise in rolling back odometers...a practice known as clocking. He could foist the cars as *low-mileage, rich, little, old-lady who only drove to church on Sunday* models. Clocking could increase a car's wholesale value by an average of $1,000.00 on its way to the auction.

This practice continued for a considerable period of time, but after having sold hundreds of these doctored vehicles, the uncanny instincts of dirty birds and dirty deals brought the *foul* home to roost. One of the earlier sales of a *low-mileage* Cadillac went south...literally. The owner just happened to drive the vehicle downstate from where it had been purchased at auction. The vehicle just happened to need service and just happened to be taken to a local dealership, where as luck would have it, it had by coincidence been serviced before Jim had discovered it advertised for sale in the local paper.

It just so happened that the owner of the car noticed that the invoice for the service showed the vehicle's mileage as 100,000 miles more than the odometer reading. He thought the discrepancy was a clerical error, but upon inquiry learned that it just so happened that this particular car had originally been sold new by that dealer and according to the dealership's permanent maintenance records, the mileage shown on the invoice was accurate.

This epiphany triggered a lengthy investigation by the Department of Motor Vehicles, the auto auction company and a variety of law enforcement authorities to unravel the culpability of the players associated with the saga of the *low-mileage* Cadillac. Before it was over, 400 cheated car buyers were identified and the auto auction and its insurers were required to reimburse some $400,000.00 to customers. A criminal case was filed against the Norths and Jim Hewitt, charging each of them with 400 felony counts of tampering with an odometer.

This was not a new experience for Jake North. He and his son had faced legal problems before, but Jim Hewitt had never been confronted with a legal problem and didn't know what he should do. What he did know was that he needed a good lawyer and he needed one in a hurry. The only lawyer he knew personally was a man who had been attending his regular A.A. meetings for several years, showing up weekly despite the fact that he couldn't stay sober from one meeting to the next. Jim asked one of the longtime members of A.A. if he thought this lawyer could handle his criminal case. He was advised there was no better defense lawyer when he was sober, but keeping him sober might be a full-time job.

As it turned out, Jim didn't have the kind of money justified by Clyde's expertise to pay his fee. However he did have something that Clyde very badly needed and wanted; he had an established sobriety. They struck a deal whereby Clyde would represent Jim in his criminal case and Jim would provide two years of 24/7 bodyguard service...to protect Clyde from himself and separate him from the bottle. Jim moved in with Clyde, bag and baggage, home and office, as a constant companion and custodian.

Clyde severed Jim's case from the case of the other defendants and filed a demurrer challenging the sufficiency of the complaint. The District Attorney had no evidence implicating Jim in a conspiracy. The financial records failed to disclose any participation by Jim in the enhanced value of the vehicles when they were sold at auction. The clocking took place after the cars Jim had located were delivered to the Norths. There was nothing illegal about the Norths paying Jim a fee for locating the type of vehicles they had specified.

The prosecutor, Sean Hazinger, a former civil lawyer, was intrigued by Clyde's arguments and tactics of using the demurrer to delay Jim's case. He was not impressed enough, however, to bring Jim's case to a conclusion. He was unconcerned about the delays occasioned by Clyde's demurrer because his case against the Norths was moving solidly forward.

The legal proceedings were not the only, nor were they the worst, of the predicaments confronting Clyde's client and the Norths. Many businesses have investors; even established legitimate business institutions like automobile auction houses. They may have individual investors who are the kind of people that don't sit back passively and tolerate the victimization of their wallets. Often those kinds of people know other kinds of people who are connected with an organization that collects debts by unconventional methods.

One of the occupational hazards of being a crook is to prey upon the wrong game. An example would be fleecing a little lamb which turns out to be a Tyrannosaurus Rex in sheep's clothing. One day the crook is in a parking lot or strolling in the park when he is casually approached by a couple of men whom he's never met, but who know his name. The two guys are hard-eyed, hard-nosed, hard-mouthed, hard-bodied and tell the crook he's not going to get away with what he stole...he's about to pay it back...in money or blood.

This is exactly what happened to Clyde's client and Papa and Junior North. Clyde took immediate pains to disassociate Jim from the Norths' misdeeds. Some of his past cases brought Clyde in contact with some people who knew some people. He was able to use that backchannel network to deliver an explanation of Jim's lack of involvement in the Norths' clocking scheme to the people who knew the people who knew the interested investors in the auto auction.

Meanwhile back in the courthouse, Clyde continued to file demurrers until the case made its way to a judge whose perception matched Clyde's comfort level. He was able to keep the case afloat with longer continuances.

In bureaucratic due course, the Department of Motor Vehicles decided to revoke Jim's dealer license. Clyde undertook the defense to save his client's livelihood as part and parcel to saving his life and liberty. He knew the most effective members of the D.M.V. staff were headquartered in Sacramento. Clyde had the case removed from the capital to the local office for administrative hearings. He subpoenaed a number of Jim's prior used-car customers, one of whom was an A.A. member who had been a prominent and powerful attorney in the U.S. Attorney's office. This gentleman's appearance on the witness stand was decisive. When Clyde asked him if he'd ever bought a used car from Jim Hewitt, he testified, "Yes...and I'd buy another one any time." The administrative law judge was obviously impressed and overwhelmingly convinced. Jim kept his license.

Jake North and his son, facing extensive prison time at a minimum and hard-guy retaliation as the maximum sentence,

21

jumped bail and went on the run. Within a year, the son was found in a shallow grave out in the desert, where the autopsy revealed he had been buried alive. Jake surfaced with his tongue cut out and a triangle of .22 caliber bullet holes in his forehead.

Throughout the entire ordeal, Jim honored his commitment to Clyde, living in his pocket and keeping him sober. He earned the privilege of presenting Clyde with his one-year *birthday* cake at the A.A. meeting, marking Clyde's first full year of sobriety.

Ultimately, as time passed, with the conclusive termination of the two principal defendants, the prosecutor became less interested and the judge got more pragmatic about the interminable demurrers prolonging Jim's criminal case. Jim was permitted to plead *no contest* to a misdemeanor infraction and got off with a $500.00 fine.

Just as the case ended, Jim presented Clyde with his two-year A.A. birthday cake and was relieved of his full-time bottle-baby-sitting job. Both Jim and Clyde were freed at the same time…Jim from his servitude to Clyde…Clyde from his dependence on the bottle.

5

Mething Around

The Hells Angels enjoyed a monopoly on the methamphetamine market until some erstwhile garage chemist in San Diego discovered that *ephedrine*, a common nasal decongestant, could be used in the place of red phosphorous as a precursor chemical in the illicit manufacture of methamphetamine.

In no time at all, San Diego became the meth capital of the world. It was easy to hold that distinction as long as *ephedrine* was readily available.

Several states began closing down on the legal sources of the ephedrine, severely limiting the supply. Florida and Utah were among the last states to shut down the availability of the substance.

Squirrel had been a truck driver for most of his life. He observed the drug problems of his kids, but he never considered himself to be involved in the drug culture that was sweeping the country. But even a blind squirrel finds the odd acorn. Squirrel's eyes were always wide open to any opportunity to improve his lot. When he learned a commonly used antihistamine, ephedrine, was a highly sought after ingredient in the illegal manufacture of illicit methamphetamine, he reasoned that he could gain a monopoly on ephedrine and control the entire meth market.

At the time, the price of ephedrine was $1,000.00 a pound. Squirrel intended to corner the market and raise the price to $10,000.00 a pound. When he began his quest, the total inventory of legitimately used ephedrine in the United States was 8,000 pounds. At the time of his arrest, he was in possession of 3,365 pounds, nearly half of the nation's legitimate supply.

At the time, ephedrine was emerging as a drug to be placed on the controlled substances list. However, conspiracy to manufacture methamphetamine by whatever method could bring a sentence of enough years to amount to life imprisonment.

The DEA in its zeal to claim the bust ahead of their competitors in the other drug enforcement agencies, rushed to get a search warrant. They served it without their drug-sniffing dogs, a mistake that resulted in their finding no illegal drugs in their search. Nevertheless, they snared Squirrel and his wife with a massive amount of ephedrine, which was not yet illegal per se.

After his arrest, Squirrel had a friend contact Clyde. Considering Squirrel's age and lack of criminal record, Clyde visited him at the MCC, the Federal prison tower in San Diego, and immediately recognized the merits of the case. Squirrel had squirreled away an enormous amount of cash in a number of safe deposit boxes which had not yet come to the attention of the government. In addition, Squirrel was possessed of encyclopedic knowledge of the inner workings of the interstate meth market.

The Assistant United States Attorney assigned to the case, wanted life sentences for Squirrel and his wife and attempted to block every effort to obtain Squirrel's release on bail. However, at the detention hearing pursued by the Government to avoid bail in violation of the Eighth Amendment to the U.S. Constitution, the Magistrate granted bail anyway. Clyde had arranged for 29 of Squirrel's salt-of-the-earth relatives to personally pledge their life savings, nearly five million dollars' worth of property, to secure his court appearance bond. This was more than adequate for the Magistrate, much to the frustration of the Assistant U.S. Attorney.

Further into the investigation of the case, it was determined that the tentacles of Squirrel's network reached past

Utah into Florida. Additional inquiry resulted in a determination that the primary cause of action lay in Florida. Clyde and Squirrel traveled to Florida to meet with the DEA agents and their supervisors. They learned that one entire DEA group out of Miami was dedicated just to actions to interdict the manufacture and distribution of Methamphetamine.

Squirrel's knowledge of the speed industry ran so deep that the specter of his cooperation emerged as an obvious opportunity for the DEA. He was like a dream come true. Despite that, the exuberance of the DEA and anxiety they displayed at the idea of Squirrel's cooperation struck a dissonant note in Clyde's suspicious mind. Putting that alert on hold, Clyde instigated a plan to have the DEA agents in Florida convince the DEA agents in San Diego to allow Squirrel to become a cooperating defendant. The San Diego agents were unimpressed and unwilling to cooperate. Over the objections of the San Diego DEA and the Assistant U.S. Attorney, Clyde successfully brokered a cooperative relationship with the Florida DEA.

As a result of the Florida arrangement, the U.S. Attorney in San Diego had to ultimately dismiss his cases, without prejudice, pending the results in Florida. Clyde immediately made a deal allowing a Federal Rule 40 plea to be entered in Florida, which mandated sentencing to occur in San Diego, but under the direction and in consideration of what the Florida authorities determined was appropriate. This effectively neutered the San Diego Assistant U.S. Attorney, rendering him impotent to do anything other than to become a spokesman for the Florida prosecutors. Keeping the Florida prosecutors happy was relatively easy.

Squirrel's continued cooperation was overwhelming. One of the conditions of his bail was an agreement to surrender 39 pounds of pure ephedrine. Clyde and his investigator picked it up on a Friday afternoon, unbelievably in the midst of a different police surveillance operation. Clyde loaded the five-gallon containers into his pickup truck under the watchful eyes of a number of cops, without them questioning what was going on. He drove a small fortune in drugs through the police lines without their knowledge and without their concern.

Clyde and his investigator then proceeded to the DEA office to turn over the ephedrine as agreed in the conditions of Squirrel's bail. The only problem was that the DEA was in TGIF party mode and the office was closed. Repeated calls to the mobile phones of the numerous agents produced only one response from an inebriated agent. He accepted the containers, but forgot to refrigerate them. Left un-refrigerated over the weekend, the ephedrine lost 30% of its weight by volume due to evaporation.

On Monday morning, The Assistant U.S. Attorney was demanding, "Where's the rest of the dope?" He hauled Squirrel before a U.S. Magistrate to revoke his bail. Clyde produced San Diego's foremost forensic chemist to testify as to the evaporation of ephedrine overnight, not to mention what would happen over a three-day weekend if left un-refrigerated. The Magistrate agreed that the condition of bail had been met and affirmed Squirrel's release.

Thereafter, while courteously hat-tipping to the San Diego Assistant U.S. Attorney, almost all of Clyde's legal maneuvering was concentrated on the Assistant U.S. Attorney in Florida. He had never experienced Clyde's virtuosity in the art of slide-step criminal case choreography.

Clyde went to Miami with Squirrel to meet with all of the DEA agents. They devised a plan whereby Squirrel would allegedly buy ephedrine from a number of dealers in Southern California and sell to other dealers in Florida. The government supplied a humongous quantity of ephedrine for Squirrel to sell. He disposed of it in a very short period of time.

Clyde's uneasiness with the Florida DEA agents was still festering in the back of his mind. He sensed there was something amiss...just couldn't put his finger on it. A considerable number of deals were transacted until a situation arose where Squirrel had possession of $30,000.00 of drug money in cash which he was to turn over to the DEA. Squirrel gave the money to Clyde, who called the DEA in Florida to ask for instructions for transferring the cash. He was instructed to mail the cash to Florida instead of turning it in to the local DEA office. Clyde questioned not only the total irresponsibility, but the incredible stupidity of mailing cash. Instead of complying with the instructions, Clyde bought a number of cashier's checks made payable to the DEA agent in Florida from the Oceanside branch of California's largest bank. He mailed the checks to the agent and then waited and watched.

Ten days later, a trace on the cashier's checks revealed that the DEA agent had washed the money through a sham bank account and kept the money for himself. This was the beginning of the end in the prosecution of the case of U.S. vs. Squirrel. Clyde became the ring master of a circus involving the various Government agencies.

He scheduled a debriefing session in San Diego for 1:30 in the afternoon, believing the DEA agents would all interrupt their lunch to attend so they could hear what revelations Squirrel would disclose. Clyde instructed Squirrel to arrive early, and while all of the agents were waiting to be debriefed, he and Squirrel's wife…un-tailed for the first time since the original arrests…went to all of the banks and emptied the safe deposit boxes full of Squirrel's hidden cash. With all of the currency safely tucked away in Clyde's safe, he and Mrs. Squirrel arrived at the debriefing a half-hour late…no one asked why.

The circus acts were performed for the DEA in both Florida and California, each time pulling back the safety nets from under the drug agents' flying trapeze. Then it was time for the main event in the center ring. First, Clyde informed the U.S. Attorney's office in San Diego that something was fishy in Florida. He produced copies of the $30,000.00 worth of cashier's checks that had ended up in the personal account of the DEA Agent. This revelation caused a tsunami of reactions across the country. The sticky-fingered agent in Florida was placed on permanent administrative leave at DEA Headquarters in Washington, D.C. His boss in Florida, who had structured the money-laundering embezzlement operation for the benefit of his whole group, was sentenced to two years in Federal prison for tax evasion.

Squirrel's cooperation case was transferred to San Diego, where his criminal case had already been dismissed. Guidance for the sentencing in the Florida cooperation case was to have been provided by the prosecutors in Florida, but since the Florida prosecution fell apart as a result of the scandal, San Diego was left holding a very thin file in Squirrel's case with no guidance from the Florida prosecutors.

Then, Squirrel's team hit another homerun. The California DEA was allowed to seize $125,000.00 cash which Squirrel had for the purchase of ephedrine, but only $105,000.00 found its way into the official coffers. The DEA supervisor was unable to account for the missing $20,000.00. He was banished to Bangkok.

Clyde kept performing the circus acts for three more years of wire-walking, hoop-jumping and clown tumbling before Squirrel was finally scheduled for sentencing. The hearing took place behind the closed doors of the judge's chambers, without embarrassing press coverage. What began as a possible double lifetime-sentence for Mr. and Mrs. Squirrel ended as a dismissal of all charges against the wife and three years of probation and a fifty dollar fine for Squirrel.

After the conclusion of the case, Clyde sent Squirrel a bill for the remaining balance of his fee in the amount of $10,000.00. The bill came back with a note scrawled across it: *FUCK YOU CLYDE!* Well, at least he took the time to write and put a stamp on the envelope.

Squirrel died of cancer 10 years later. Five years after his death, his son, Squirrel, Jr., was charged with a robbery in Colorado. He called Clyde and asked that he defend him. Clyde politely declined.

6
Scars are for Healing

Manny was from Detroit. His brother died of brain cancer shortly after the death of their father. That left him as the lone surviving male in the family. Only his mother and two sisters remained. Manny had a severe methamphetamine addiction when he left Motown to the dismay of his family. He landed in San Diego where he crashed in crack house…a typical drug-addict rat's nest.

Heavily and totally hooked on meth, it was known to his suppliers that he was helplessly willing to do anything to get a fix. He was constantly used and abused by drug dealers as a delivery mule, a bagman, a throwaway fall guy and frontal target, who would have no rip-off ambitions. His sole mission in life was to get more meth.

One of the dealers who regularly exploited Manny had negotiated a deal to buy a huge quantity of ephedrine, an essential ingredient in the manufacture of methamphetamine. He decided that Manny would be the person who would carry the bag containing $800,000.00 in U.S. currency when the purchase took place. For good measure, the dealer placed a loaded and cocked .45 caliber semiautomatic pistol on top of the money in the bag.

Manny had no compunctions about being used in dangerous drug deals. His only thoughts were about the meth and how much more he could get later if he survived. Actually he didn't really care about surviving anymore without his drugs.

The dealer carefully planned and refined his arrangements to acquire the ephedrine, so that the deal would go smoothly with no snags. He considered every contingency. He and Manny would go into the restaurant where the exchange was to take place. Another of his cohorts would be waiting and watching outside in the car, while yet another co-conspirator would be standing outside on the street as his early warning system if anything went wrong.

Where the dealer miscalculated was that the problem didn't come from the outside…it came instead from the inside. The drugs he was buying were being sold by the DEA in a reverse scam on the common practice of a *buy* bust. However, the penalties for the perpetrators were the same whether they were selling or buying. Then, there was the added factor of the loaded weapon at the scene, which substantially increased the penalty for each of the participants…in this particular case, more than 30 years in prison for each of them.

Shortly after Manny's arrest, his family in Detroit learned of his plight and contacted an Assistant U.S. Attorney whom they knew in California. As it turned out, the case was being handled in his own office by a female colleague. He also knew of Clyde's successful record in other similar cases. On the condition of strict anonymity, he recommended that the family call Clyde.

Manny's widowed mother and two sisters arrived at Clyde's office prepared to do whatever possible to assist Manny. They paid Clyde's fee and pledged their home to secure bail without complaint. Clyde visited Manny in the Federal lockup and immediately became aware of the wounds on Manny's body left by his excessive use of methamphetamines. He realized that his first job would be to save Manny's life, which was in great jeopardy from the ravages of the drugs he had consumed.

There was no way Manny could get healthy in jail and would likely not survive incarceration with his addiction untreated and uncontrolled. Prisons are among the easiest places to acquire illegal drugs. Smuggling drugs into these institutions is a commonplace activity of the prison gangs with ties to gang members not currently serving time. Controlling the availability of get-high contraband behind the prison walls plays a major role in the gangs' power.

Clyde's first objective was to get Manny out on bail. He decided that the best approach would be to attack the Government in its most vulnerable spot. He determined that the softest spot, as unorthodox and unconventional as it seemed, was the lead DEA agent. He was very youthful looking for someone in his advanced position. This indicated to Clyde that he was probably a smart self-starter and a more independent thinker than most. Based on his apparent age, he could not have been on the job for very long. Clyde hoped that he might still have a vestige of optimistic humanity remaining in his sole, and had not yet been converted to an adamant cynic by a career immersed in a losing battle with a pool of drug-dreg miscreants.

Clyde engaged the DEA agent in non-adversarial conversations about the horrors of addiction and drug use. He confessed his earlier alcoholism to support his knowledge of the ravages of addiction from his personal experiences fighting his demons and how finding sobriety saved his own life. He moved the conversation to how wonderful it would be if *they*…he and the agent…could jointly be responsible for getting Manny clean…even if it required a lengthy stretch behind bars.

Eventually, Clyde convinced the DEA agent to agree to releasing Manny on bail if he were placed in a rehab ranch way out in the country east of San Diego, which had a history of success detoxifying alcoholics and addicts, and weaning them from their addictions. The folks at the ranch agreed to inform the DEA if Manny eloped or failed to remain drug and alcohol free according to the facility's strict supervision and testing policies.

Next, Clyde went to work on the Assistant U.S. Attorney, suggesting that Manny might be available to testify for the Government if he could become clean and sober to enhance his credibility. Once having planted the seed in the prosecutor's mind, he backed off to let the idea percolate in her head.

The other three defendants had hired their own lawyers. One of them was approaching his client's case by attempting to have him declared insane and committed to a mental institution.

Shortly after the cases began, one of the other attorneys was himself committed to a mental institution. The third lawyer, who was from out of town, couldn't seem to get to the court appearances on time and was fired by his client. Some of the replacement attorneys didn't last very long either, causing the prosecutor considerable frustration and creating chaos with her efforts to manage the Government's case.

The Assistant U.S. Attorney was a competent and experienced prosecutor. She was neither ambitiously hard nor naively soft. She happened to be in the throes of disentanglement from her first husband, who also happened to be an Assistant U.S. Attorney, and arranging to marry her current entanglement, who also happened to be another Assistant U.S. Attorney. Knowing that she had more than enough personal and professional aggravation in her life, Clyde used a comfy, sympathetic, big-brother approach to appeal to her sensitive side and offer some help to relieve some of the pressure of her professional dilemma.

He pointed out that he was the only defense lawyer in the case who was always prepared and always could be depended upon. He seized upon these circumstances and offered to help her get some resolution in the case. Clyde persuaded her to accept an agreement that after Manny got clean and sober, he would testify against the other co-defendants in return for a sentence commensurate with the value of his testimony and the recommendation of the lead DEA agent...she agreed. She knew that the sentences would be in excess of 30 years.

So, Manny got his bail and went into rehab, where he immediately embraced the idea of sobriety and threw himself willingly into the program. Clyde maintained close contact with the lead DEA agent and made a point of always telling him about Manny's enthusiastic progress at the rehab ranch. In his report, Manny's probation officer indicated that in his experience he had never seen a worse case of meth addiction. His body was riddled with needle scars and his daily usage had been off the charts.

Despite the positive probation reports and Manny's successful progress, the Federal sentencing guidelines at that time required a recommendation of 33 years in prison for the crimes. The only way a defendant could qualify for a lesser sentence was under Rule 5K1, which permitted a reduction of the sentence commensurate with the value of the substantial assistance provided by the defendant to the Government in its prosecution of the case.

As things played out, each of the other defendants pled guilty and Manny was never required to testify. Although his plea and sentencing bargain remained in force, he actually had rendered no substantial assistance, but had only agreed that he would. Therefore, his entitlement to the reduced sentence benefit was questionable.

Clyde began carefully crafting a phased series of letters to the Assistant U.S. Attorney underscoring the assistance Manny's agreement to testify had actually rendered. He pointed out that the other three defendants might not have pleaded guilty but for Manny's imminent cooperation. Clyde also reminded her of his own cooperation by enduring, rather than exploiting the chaos occasioned by the inadequacies of the other defense attorneys. Ultimately, the Assistant U.S. Attorney agreed to file the 5K1 motion.

What remained was for Clyde to negotiate a favorable sentence recommendation from the DEA agent which the Assistant U.S. Attorney had earlier agreed to accept. In court, at the sentencing hearing, he approached the lead DEA agent who was sitting in an aisle seat. Clyde knelt beside him and quietly inquired what sentence he thought Manny should serve at the rehab ranch. This friendly little conversation clearly reminded the agent of the success Manny had achieved at the facility and how the opportunity his continued participation in the program would contribute to his full rehabilitation.

The young Fed asked, "How about three years?"

Clyde relayed the proposed recommendation to the prosecutor who had no objection. It was presented to the Court, which accepted the recommendation as being consistent with the intent of Rule 5K1.

The end result was that after the initial 29 days in the Federal lockup and three years at the Rehab Ranch, during which Manny became the institution's assistant manager, Manny was free, but reluctant to leave the place that had saved his life. During his residence at the ranch, as a part of the recovery program, he had taken a correspondence course in cinematography and had been offered a job in Hollywood. He succeeded in his chosen field and by the time he reached his forties, he had a family and a home in Los Angeles. His co-defendants were still languishing in prison with more than half their sentences remaining to be served.

Many legal loopholes result from forced or unforced errors committed by prosecutors. Many more result from precedents established in prior cases. Others occur because of a failure to follow established rules and procedures. But in this case, there was a procedural opportunity like Rule 5K1. Knowing of its existence and refusing to be detoured because of the way the case was resolved allowed Clyde to play the hand he was dealt and through meticulous cultivation of the human factors create his own loophole. He took advantage of the humanity he sensed in the prosecutor and the DEA agent who still believed in the value to society of rehabilitation over incarceration. It didn't hurt that he had a client who deserved a second chance.

7
Money Counts

armon was the black sheep of an otherwise wealthy and well-respected family from Montecito, the most exclusive suburb of the classy community of Santa Barbara. He had wandered around aimlessly and wasted his life until he started working for the owner of a junkyard. Because his boss, Warner, had other business interests, Harmon thought he had found a job with an unlimited future. They had been successfully dealing small amounts of marijuana for quite some time.

Late one Saturday afternoon, Harmon got a call from Warner, who announced he had scored an enormous deal. Harmon was to bring their cash stash to Denver for the largest buy in their pot-peddling careers.

First, Warner explained to Harmon where in the junkyard he had deposited their investment capital. Some was hidden in the trunk of a '59 Cadillac, some under the hood of a '49 Ford and the rest in a 55-gallon drum in the bed of an old Dodge pickup truck. All told, Harmon dug out just over a million dollars in used bills. A lot of their profits had been squirreled away, awaiting the opportunity to buy into the big-time.

Warner had set up a meeting for noon the next day, Sunday, at the famous Brown Hotel in Denver. Harmon had to figure a way to get there with the money bundle in only about sixteen hours. Fearing flat tires, radar traps, and falling asleep at the wheel, Harmon ruled out driving. Santa Barbara to Denver was just too long a trip. He decided the best thing to do was fly. However, getting through airports in a rush with a duffel-bag full of cash was another problem, so he decided to charter a plane.

Harmon found the owner of a nice, small, private rental jet flying out of Los Angeles, who was willing to leave at 2:00 a.m. on a Sunday morning. He would arrive in Denver at dawn...and for a mere six thousand dollars.

Of course, the charter jet people didn't bother Harmon with the details of having to file a flight plan and comply with other FAA regulations. Paying for the service in $6,000.00 of old currency got all the red flags flying before the jet's door was closed. A signal went up in the Federal network and Harmon was marked for surveillance before the wheels lifted off the tarmac.

Harmon took a cab directly from the Denver airport to the Brown Hotel to meet Warner for breakfast. Warner outlined the career-making deal he had arranged for a huge quantity of high-test-quality marijuana at a cut-rate price. Harmon would wait in one room of the hotel with the money while Warner met the big dealers in another. When everything was set, Warner would telephone Harmon to bring in the cash.

Warner was blinded by the excitement of this long-awaited opportunity to become a hot-shot dealer just like the hotshot dealers with whom he was dealing. The hotshot dealers, whom he so envied, were actually hotshot DEA agents. They possessed a vast amount of the highest quality weed...and why not? They had seized it from the very best traffickers they had previously busted.

The DEA's only goal was to strike a deal to sell the marijuana to Warner and when it was consummated, arrest Warner and Harmon and seize their money as evidence. Later they would confiscate the money under the forfeiture provisions of the existing law.

For quite some time, the Government had been lobbying for an easy way to grab and retain drug money. They finally succeeded in having a new regulation issued which allowed for the instant forfeiture of the money at the moment it was offered in payment for the drugs. Regardless of any laws to the contrary, this was the procedure they had been relying upon ever since President Nixon's program for the IRS to seize the money had been knocked down in the 1976 case of U.S. vs. Laing.

According to their newly established rules, Warner and Harmon would be imprisoned for ten years to life, the Government would instantly be a million dollars richer and the marijuana would be returned to the DEA vaults to be recycled as sucker-bait in the next sting operation.

Everything was being secretly videotaped when Warner met with the DEA *dealers* and Harmon came in on cue to display the cash. Then, surprisingly, the Government agents said the actual delivery would take place in Corpus Christi, Texas. They did this because they wanted to move the crime across state lines so the interstate conspiracy laws would assure exclusive Federal jurisdiction. This little maneuver allowed the Feds to avoid a complicated state felony action and preempt any claim on the money by the State authorities.

In their overabundance of greed, however, the DEA hotshots encountered a series of unanticipated events which resulted in a crash landing. Harmon and Warner were so enraptured by the vision of being propelled into cannabis-venders' Nirvana, that they readily agreed to travel from Colorado to Texas and consummate the deal at 5:00 p.m. the next day.

They had plenty of time to arrange for getting their money aboard a regularly scheduled commercial airliner as luggage. Since the DEA had secretly smoothed the way, they had no difficulty getting the money aboard the aircraft. The DEA agents had arranged the meeting at a nearly vacant hotel in Corpus Christi. Not having time to organize deployment of other DEA agents to work the sting, they had called on the local police department's narcotics squad to assist as backup.

As it happened, the Corpus Christi narcs were involved in another bust that day and did not even get notified until midday that they were expected to help the DEA later that afternoon. Not wanting to appear unprepared in the face of the almighty Federal Government, the local sheriff took six street patrolmen off their beats to handle the action.

At the appointed hour, Warner knocked on the door of the hotel room and was ushered in by the DEA/dealers...the videotape started rolling to make a record of the crime. Short of time to make preparations, the Feds had to use an unsophisticated setup of simple video equipment to create a record of the transaction. Warner, who envisioned becoming an instant big shot industrialist in the marijuana industry, didn't have the good common sense to become suspicious when he was directed to sit in an out-of-the way isolated chair in the corner of the room in line with the hidden camera...he was too focused on the dream of his imminent climb to the pinnacle of success.

Getting his cue from Warner, Harmon came in from another room and dumped all the money on the table. The drama played on as Warner and Harmon counted out a million dollars in hundred dollar bills. Despite the frantic assistance of the two DEA agents, the money count took half an hour...the videotape very nearly ran out. Finally the Feds dropped the curtain on the scene. To say that Warner and Harmon were disappointed would rank among the greatest understatements in history. Not only did they not get their pot...not only were their hopes of undreamed of success dashed...but, they got busted and hauled off to the local pokey.

At that time, the detention procedure of denying bail to suspects facing over ten years in prison had not yet been instigated. Harmon called his rich family in California, who swiftly arranged for bail. He and Warner were whisked away back to Santa Barbara scrambling to find a lawyer.

Harmon's family had a friend who was a dealer in art and antiques. He had a longtime customer and friend who happened to be a criminal defense lawyer named Clyde Munsell. Harmon wasted no time getting to Clyde's office eager to retain him to handle his case. A retainer agreement was signed and Clyde's fees were guaranteed by Harmon's family.

Knowing a case of this complexity would require particular adroitness and finesse, Clyde hired Barry Strong, a retired star of the U.S. Attorney's office in Southern California as associate counsel. Before he retired to private practice, Barry had been Clyde's favorite friendly, respected and respectful adversary in numerous Federal cases. Working together in harness, they were a pair of racing thoroughbred warhorses.

Since the most substantial of the illegal activities had occurred in Corpus Christi, Clyde and Harry journeyed to Denver, where they convinced the busy U.S. Attorney's office there to defer prosecution of the case to the U.S. Attorney in Texas. Having assured only a single venue of prosecution, Clyde and Barry moved the case and themselves to Corpus Christi.

Corpus Christi was an old, picturesque town on the coast of the Gulf of Mexico. It had many quaint, tiled buildings that were largely empty because the area's water supply had become inadequate and was literally and economically drying up. It was a place that would welcome a million dollar drug money seizure, spread around from the Feds to cooperating local agencies.

Clyde and Barry settled in and retained a local private investigator. They examined the case in detail and discovered it was not promising from the defense's point of view. The videotaped drug deal was dramatically dispositive of an open and shut case for the prosecution.

The U.S. Attorney's office in Corpus Christi had not yet presented the case to the Grand Jury. They were still busy adding up all the charges to be filed against the hapless duo of Harmon and Warner. Clearly, it would add up to a minimum sentence of ten years and likely much more. The Federal Sentencing Guidelines had just been adopted, and a drug deal for a million-dollar quantity of marijuana made the defendants eligible to be sentenced to double the prison time.

Sometime toward the end of the first week, Clyde decided to request a formal count of the cash. This was something rarely done in such cases, since the money itself was not evidence according to legal precedents. It had been seized as evidence pending the forfeiture procedure and it would have to be accounted for when it was turned over to the U.S. Treasury. But Clyde and Barry knew that the DEA was the only Government agency without audit controls. They kept no record of how much they took in…only how much they turned over to the Treasury. The DEA could not be bothered with the painstaking responsibility of keeping track of the *free* money they confiscated from criminals.

This situation stimulated the instincts of the old fraud-auditor accountant that Clyde had once been. He and Barry also knew there had long been hushed rumors, but no documentary evidence, of *shrinkage* in drug money seizures. In this case, however, there was documentary evidence of the total amount of the seized money thanks to the DEA's own videotape of the million dollars being counted out during the sting operation.

The requested formal cash count totaled only $800,000.00, with $200,000 of the money evidenced on the videotape missing. Clyde and Barry obtained the disciplinary records of each of the DEA agents and local policemen involved in the bust. Nothing showed up. However, one of the local beat cops who had been hastily called in for backup had been hired just a few months earlier, having moved to Texas from Tennessee, where he had also been on the police force.

Once the Tennessee records were obtained, it became clear the man had moved on after being questioned about a case there where $180,000.00 of a big seizure of drug money had gone missing. By itself, such circumstantial evidence would not be persuasive to a hardboiled prosecutor. However, very little additional investigation revealed the man had recently purchased an expensive automobile, which he foolishly registered in his own name and had purchased a large house in a nice suburb of Corpus Christi.

This left little doubt about what had become of the missing money, and there was little doubt how bad publicity about the *coincidence* would look. It was a case of appearance becoming the reality. It didn't take much cajoling to get the U.S. Attorney's office in Corpus Christi to agree not to pursue the case at any level...not to present it to the Grand Jury...not seek a plea bargain nor do anything else but bid Clyde and Barry bon voyage as they quietly spirited their client back to Santa Barbara, with a promise not to disclose the reason for their agreement not to pursue the case.

Meantime, back in Santa Barbara, Harmon was going crazy trying to explain to his upscale family about his pending decade in prison. Everyone was hoping for a minimum sentence. No one expected the complete vindication and Harmon's skate-free status which Clyde announced on his return. The family had arranged for the retainer fee to be paid piecemeal to Clyde through their family attorney as the case progressed. Now, that Clyde had delivered the *Get Out of Jail* card to Harmon, his family decided to pay Clyde only half the agreed fee.

This is not an unusual phenomenon. The sooner and more successfully a lawyer achieves the desired result, the less complicated and difficult his job appears, thereby depreciating the value of his services in the client's mind. So Clyde explained that if a fee dispute went to the mandated arbitration process, the attorney-client privilege might be waived. If the mutual silence deal with the U.S. Attorney became known as a result, the deal would have no more hush-up value to the prosecution. They would suffer further embarrassment, and Harmon could find he had rolled the dice and landed on *Go Directly to Jail; Do Not Pass Go; Do not collect $200.00;* and he had already used his *Get Out of Jail* card. So a compromise was reached whereby Clyde was paid a slightly reduced fee and his representation was terminated.

Since Clyde was no longer on the case, there was no one to finalize the agreement in Corpus Christi to secure the deal for wall-to-wall *no-prosecution agreements*. It should have come as no surprise, that in the absence of Federal prosecution, the State of Texas decided to go after the seized $800,000.00 and came after Harmon and Warner with state felony charges.

Fortunately for the wanna-be drug kingpin-junkmen from California, Texas was more interested in their money than their blood. The Lone Star State offered them plea bargain agreements to plead guilty in exchange for probation. Thus, Texas got the $800,000.00 and didn't have to foot the bill for their room and board in Huntsville for the next ten years.

Of course, this cost Harmon's family yet more fees than they might otherwise have paid Clyde, for a different lawyer, just to get their child prodigy lifetime identification as a convicted felon. Money certainly does count!

8

OD - DOA

Right around the time Clyde was getting sober, a friend brought him into what was then the biggest-bucks divorce case in the history of California.

Brenda and her husband, Ben, a tuna fisherman, had started with a $2,500.00 stake she acquired from a second trust deed on her home near the beach. They went on to become the superstars of the tuna industry. Their ship came in after Ben hired a lobbyist to get the price of tuna jacked up from $60.00 to $850.00 a ton. *Damn the Consumer, Full Speed Ahead!*

By the time their marriage fell apart, they had accumulated a community property estate worth two-hundred-million-dollars. They owned outright 29 of the big purse-seiner commercial tuna-fishing boats working out of San Diego.

In their heyday, Mr. and Mrs. Gardner were quite a dynamic duo. Brenda was a champion water-skier and Ben was a dashing sportsman-athlete. They were very prominent among the rich and beautiful people. Alas, Brenda had two children from her prior marriage who did not fit into their picture-perfect life.

Billy Sage was a heroin addict and Bobby Sage was an alcoholic. They proved to be the undoing of the Gaines' very gainful marriage. Brenda ended up a pill addict, while Ben cast off and sailed away.

Ben hired the biggest-league, heaviest-weight lawyer from the Los Angeles area to represent him in the divorce. Naturally, this ultra-connected mover-shaker big-fish counselor did an excellent job of intimidating an overwhelmed, alcoholic judge in the small pond of San Diego. They were able to force a settlement whereby Brenda got two million dollars...only one percent of the community property, and Ben got the rest.

By the time Clyde got the case, Brenda's prior lawyer, also a heavy-weight, bar association president, had already blown the statute of limitations. There was nothing left but to take it to the Supreme Court of the State of California, which Clyde did but ultimately lost because the statute of limitations had run. As a part of the total package, Clyde had agreed to represent her sons in their criminal cases. Within a 51-week period, Clyde handled 38 separate criminal matters for the unwise Sage boys.

The most memorable of those cases involved Billy Sage who, in addition to his drug addictions, was addicted to younger women, showering them with jewelry bought with his mother's money. One of the girls was Barbie, a lovely young 23 year old lady from New England. Billy and Barbie moved to Vail, Colorado, where his mother had just purchased the largest house in the famous ski resort-town. They were only there for a short time, when one Wednesday afternoon, Clyde received a frantic call from Billy's mother that Billy had gone on a binge, after which he killed Barbie in the Vail residence.

Clyde had to tell Brenda to forget trying to get Billy off. The case against him was grim and he already had five prior felony convictions. At best, he could expect a life sentence when convicted under the *little bitch* habitual offender statute in Colorado. However, Brenda insisted Clyde help her son and convinced Clyde that Billy was worth helping.

Vail had earlier become infamous when singer/actress Claudine Longet, ex-wife of top-pop crooner Andy Williams, killed her boyfriend, Spyder Savitch. She ultimately pled guilty to a fourth degree homicide, a misdemeanor in Colorado, and got a sentence of 30 days in jail. A good deal for Claudine, but she wasn't a serial felon like Clyde's client, nor was her victim anything remotely similar to a dewy young thing like Barbie.

Clyde and his investigator flew to Denver the day after the homicide and drove a rental car to Vail, arriving there on Friday afternoon. Clyde met with Billy and sorted out the sordid facts of the case. It seemed that Billy believed Barbie was having an affair with another druggie. So, he decided to shoot her up with a fatal *hot shot mixture* of cocaine and heroin. Finding he did not have enough drugs to fulfill his little plan, he took an elephant rifle which he had stolen to his drug dealer's house and used it to blow open the front door. Once inside, at elephant-gunpoint he stole cocaine, heroin, and whatever else he could find.

After committing this armed robbery, he went home and mixed up a drug concoction, then injected himself and Barbie, supposedly with her consent. Maybe he hadn't known the cocaine had been cut with rat poison. The dosage was so lethal both of them were near death when Billy called the poison control center and asked what to do. They told him what to do and he immediately treated himself, but conveniently waited before doing the same for Barbie. She died twelve hours later due to the strychnine-laced overdose, which curled her body up like a potato chip.

Then, after hiding all the cocaine in a snow bank outside of the residence, Billy called the police and let them come get him. When Billy was arrested, the only drugs to be found were in his body. Normally possession of drugs is charged when there are some drugs to seize for evidence, so the police could only charge him with being under the influence. The police did nothing about the dead "overdosed" Barbie, except take her body to the coroner's office.

Clyde hurriedly arranged Billy's bail on the under the influence charge and got him out of jail later that day. They went to the residence, where Billy gave Clyde the drugs he had concealed in the snow bank. Clyde's investigator, in the course of doing whatever it is that investigators do, learned that the county coroner was a practicing alcoholic. Clyde decided his investigator should interview the coroner the next day, and take two quarts of premium Kentucky Bourbon whiskey as a small token of appreciation for his time.

By midnight both quarts were empty and the autopsy on Barbie was scant. The coroner forgot to open up the brain to determine the time of death, or to measure the angle of the needle puncture, which could have indicated whether she injected herself or if someone else, namely Billy, injected her.

The next day was Sunday, and Clyde arranged for the coroner to release Barbie's body so it could be transported immediately to her parents, all the way back east. On Monday, when the authorities came to work on the case, it was already over; they just didn't realize it yet.

Deputy D.A. Chet, who was an excellent lawyer, but with some notable idiosyncrasies, was in charge of the case. He and his wife lived 45 miles away from the County Courthouse, in a cabin without a telephone. Thus, the police had not notified him of Barbie's death until Monday morning. By that time, Barbie's body was already in a funeral parlor in her New England home town.

Clyde and his private sleuth had been sizing up the opposition. They discovered that almost the whole police force was inexperienced because the typical longevity of an officer in the Vail disorganization was about six weeks. The cops were greener than the forests around Vail. A survey of bars in the vicinity revealed the local consumption of cocaine was, if anything, even greater than the consumption of alcohol. Clyde and his private eye soon developed knowledgeable contacts, including one material informant, a girl who knew the drug business in town well, including the dealer Billy had ripped off in the elephant gun episode.

It had been a few days since Billy had his last fix and he started asking for the drugs he'd given up from the snow bank, "so he could sell it to a biker gang and see how many he could kill." While those drugs could have been a perfect defense to murder, they clearly meant a slam-dunk conviction for Billy under the habitual offender statutes. A conviction would result in a life-sentence with a twelve year minimum. Clyde and his shamus decided the drugs would be safer in Denver and took them there on the following Tuesday morning.

On their way to Denver, they saw a newspaper headline trumpeting the prosecution of one of the home-town, fair-haired, golden-boy defense attorneys of The Mile High City. He was charged with possession of 1/432 gram of cocaine. Since this was less than the measurable amount needed for a possession charge, it was obvious the Denver D.A. wanted to cook the goose of that particular lawyer because he was a successful adversary. When Clyde and his gumshoe drove into the D.A.'s jurisdiction with Billy's big stash of drugs, they got warm fuzzy feelings about what that champion of justice would do to an out-of-state lawyer and his accomplice in possession of such a colossal drug stash.

In those days Colorado had no branch banks, so the bulky bundle of drugs and paraphernalia went into safe deposit boxes in magnificent, imperial-tomb style vaults below two major financial institutions. Boxes were chosen for their proximity to the rest rooms in case of an emergency. They could at least make an attempt to flush the evidence. Of course, unlike a hardcore metropolitan police force, the cops in Vail had no idea that such things went on, nor did they have the professional competence to anticipate or even imagine the possibility.

Upon their return from Denver, Clyde tried to console Billy by explaining that his drugs needed to be preserved to use in his defense, so he could not have them back to kill bikers. Billy could not understand this frustrating concept and did not like it.

Shortly after they got back to California, Clyde got a call from their material informant that she learned there was a contract out on her life related to other cocaine deals in Vail. She asked Clyde to smuggle her away to San Diego. Clyde got her out of Vail and handed her over to Brenda, who stashed her in a Point Loma hotel for two months. The perils of her alcoholism required constant monitoring. In time, she became much easier to control and quite helpful.

Billy also came back to San Diego, and began a felony-of-the-week crime spree. Once it was for trying to sell stolen cars in Mexico. Another time he tried to stab somebody in a fancy restaurant men's room but only managed to stumble onto his own blade. Billy helped keep Clyde busy, as if the Vail case were not enough.

The first three hearings in Colorado did not require Billy's appearance. They involved a lot of maneuvering by Clyde, looking for cracks and wedges to find a way out. Deputy D.A., Chet, realizing his case was already badly flawed, did not want to show any of his cards. Clyde continued to offer every kind of plea bargain imaginable, including a Mexican felony, but to no avail. Eventually, the process showed the D.A. was not, like so many others, locked into his ego with a siege mentality...his lock could be opened if the right key were found.

Amazingly, it was Billy who picked the lock. Somehow, he was able to entice Barbie's sister to become his new girlfriend. The nineteen-year-old damsel suddenly became adorned with $40,000 worth of fine gold jewelry purchased with Brenda's money. Things went well for a while, as Billy and his dead victim's sister were thinking of marriage. Alas, it became obvious something was amiss with Billy's new miss, even though she did not make any of Barbie's fatal mistakes.

The day of reckoning arrived and Billy finally had to grace the court with his appearance. Clyde decided to take along an expert drug consultant. He hired a dealer-guru who had once spent 19 months on death row but got off because he was smart enough to hire an appellate ace. The guru knew how to handle things on the flight to Colorado when Billy got unruly, because he needed a heroin fix.

But, things didn't go so well at the Denver airport. Billy spilled his entire outfit...needle, syringe, rubber tourniquet, cooking spoon, dope packet and the rest of his paraphernalia on the marble concourse floor. Clyde's XXXL-size investigator managed to drop his XXXL raincoat over it. Barbie's sister decoyed security until Mr. XXXL got Billy's kit bundled inside his raincoat. Then he took over, bamboozle-schmoozing security, handing the raincoat to the sister, who took it right into the sanctuary of the little girl's room. Finally, the fictionalized account of the confusion over the cover-up satisfied those concerned and everybody ended up walking away.

Billy's outfit had been dumped in the ladies, room, so he immediately started to get cold-turkey anxiety, badly needing to have his next fix. During the drive from the airport, he began screaming he needed to get to a hospital...*not for treatment, but probably so he could steal a needle.* This didn't work, but the vehicle had to pull over; Billy bolted and ran away. Clyde caught him crossing a playground and tied him up with a tether-ball line. He remained hogtied for many miles from Denver, until there was nowhere worth running to.

The next day was no better. Billy bolted when he found out he was going to court. He knew that as a five-time loser he could very well never come back. When Clyde caught him this time, he didn't tie him up...he beat the living crap out of him. Head bloodied and bowed, Billy went to court. The matter had not yet gone to a superior court level and the local magistrate still handling the matter had glasses so thick he could barely read. Perhaps he didn't notice Billy's bruises or Clyde's skinned knuckles, or maybe he didn't care, but he continued Billy's bail so everyone could return to San Diego.

After the hearing, Clyde explored the keyhole in the case through which everyone could exit permanently. He visited Deputy D.A. Chet and suggested a plea bargain to a fourth degree misdemeanor, thus avoiding all possible habitual offender penalties He would get Billy to plead guilty and accept a maximum sentence and fines on the misdemeanor, provided the sentence would be suspended under a *sundowner* provision requiring Billy to get out of Colorado immediately and not return during a two year probation term.

While arguing this proposal, Deputy D.A. Chet, was interrupted by a telephone call. Clyde had arranged for Barbie's family to call Chet to say they were fearful Billy would harm Barbie's little sister, now his new girlfriend. They begged and pleaded with Chet to make some arrangement whereby their younger daughter could be returned to them.

By then, court hours were over, so Chet had no chance to revoke Billy's bail that day. Chet had to worry that Billy was free to leave town with Barbie's little sister, and he might eventually end up having to tell already grieving parents how he failed to protect their baby girl from the chronic criminal who was responsible for their older daughter's death. If that happened, not only would his conscience be stricken, he could even have to deal with ethical questions...problems of prosecutorial malpractice.

Chet made the *sundowner* deal with Clyde. Clyde was happy to agree to a requirement that Billy not see Barbie's sister for 38 days.

Clyde did not explain the part about the 38-day separation until they were all on the road, well away from Vail. Billy went berserk and attacked Clyde, who was in the front passenger seat while his investigator was driving. Clyde jumped over the seat into the back of the car and once again beat the crap out of Billy. Then he directed his investigator to pull over at the next place with a phone. He called Brenda to explain he'd gotten her son out of the little murder problem in Vail, but was charging an extra $10,000 in fees for having to beat up Billy twice as the only way to keep him under control. Brenda laughed, and actually did pay the additional fee.

Barbie's sister went back to New England and never came back. Billy forgot about her immediately, losing no time getting into more and more trouble. Clyde's first homicide case since he had become sober ended with an excellent result for everyone…everyone except Barbie.

9
War Whoop Lineup

Damon was the picture of a California surfer...long, flowing, straight blond hair, clear, blue eyes; fair complexion and evenly tanned. Somehow he went astray of his girlfriend, Marjorie, who gave him the gate. This sent Damon over the edge and he began what was to become a two-week alcoholic bender. His drinking continued to the point of deliriums and he began to see those subconscious demons that lurk in the depths of intoxication.

Somewhere along the line, he passed a costume store and purchased an Indian get-up, complete with feather headdress, buckskin vest, beaded breeches, and tomahawk. He took refuge in the wilds of a landscaped island at a gasoline station. No one seemed to care that a delirious, imitation Indian was camping in the bushes.

Things were fine for the first day or so, until Bob and his girlfriend, Diane drove up to the outer gas pumps. Unfortunately for Diane, she had some faint resemblance to Marjorie, much to the irate eye of drunken Damon, who was deep in his Indian delusion.

While Bob was pre-paying for his gas at the counter inside, Damon attacked. Before Bob received his change, Damon swooped out of the bushes, uttering a screeching war-whoop, and dragged Diane to the pavement. There he stabbed her several times with his hunting knife, then slashed her neck, and was trying to scalp her when interrupted by the uproar of other gas station customers. Damon fled, still whooping loudly.

Very soon, the police issued an all-points bulletin for an Indian with a bloody knife and buckskins, a description difficult to mistake...Damon was quickly arrested a few blocks away behind the dumpster at one of his regular bars. Luckily, Diane survived and did not even lose her hair.

Several days after his arraignment, since Damon was facing life imprisonment for attempted murder, assault with great bodily harm, and a host of other charges, his boss thought he should get a lawyer and not rely on the public defender's office.

Two weeks after the incident, Attorney Clyde Munsell visited Damon in jail and listened to his version of what happened. Damon, in custody, and by then, sober and much subdued, was able to see a very grim future for himself. Other things being equal, if he survived the brutal gangland of prison, he might get released in time to draw Social Security.

The DA's office dutifully filed all the obviously available charges plus the kitchen sink. Clyde moved for a line-up, to see if the witnesses would recognize Damon since he wouldn't be looking like an Indian.

The lineup was assigned to a Sergeant of the Sheriff's Department. He received Damon from the cells at 6:00 a.m. on lineup day, found five other would-be-surfer look-alikes, and explained the lineup procedure to all of them. Each would be dressed in jail coveralls and come onto a stage such that each of the witnesses could view them. Also in the lineup room was Clyde as Damon's lawyer and Clyde's private investigator along with various police, prosecutors, press, and the witnesses.

The Sergeant told Clyde the lineup would start at 10:00 a.m., noting there were two eyewitnesses, the victim and her boyfriend. Clyde asked if the lineups would be consecutive, one immediately following the other, for the two witnesses. The Sergeant said that would not be necessary, he wasn't going to waste time doing two lineups…both witnesses could be present at one time. Clyde asked the Sergeant if he was sure that was proper. "I know what I'm doing!" retorted the Sergeant, "This is my jail, counselor."

They were in the County Jail, the Sheriff Department's turf, where the Sergeant was in control. Clyde minded his place and he and his investigator just waited in the lineup room. The Sergeant placed Bob, who was one witness, in the left front row of the audience, just where the lineup subjects would enter the stage. The victim, Diane, together with the lady district attorney prosecuting the case, sat fifty feet away in the right rear of the audience. Clyde and his investigator sat in the middle of the room.

The first three subjects to enter on the lineup stage…all blond, blue-eyed, fair-skinned but tanned…got no response from the audience. The fourth to enter was Damon, and no sooner had he set foot on the stage when Bob jumped out of his seat, screaming "That's him! That's him! That son-of-a-bitch is the guy that stabbed my girl!"

What happened next was a continuation of botched police procedure. No further subjects were called to the stage. The lights went on and all the participants were excused. Everybody started talking at once except Clyde and his investigator, who just looked at each other and smiled. Of course, Bob's outburst in the presence of the victim had tainted and invalidated the identification of the suspect. The prosecutor had allowed the creation of a Constitutional defense as a result of the improper line-up procedures.

Clyde filed a motion to dismiss the case on the grounds of the lack of protection under the right to confront witnesses, due to the bungled lineup procedure. The District Attorney's office was blanching at the certainty of automatically losing a conviction for a 40- year sentence because a Sheriff's Sergeant tried to save a half-hour of his time. Clyde offered the DA a guilty plea on one lesser count, conditional on a sentence of probation only.

As a result, Damon found sobriety abruptly and completely; he never took another drink nor committed another felony. Twelve years later, he called Clyde with thanks for the path to a new, worthwhile and productive life.

It can only be imagined what the Office of the District Attorney had to say to the Sheriff's Department. Presumably the Sergeant also got his future straightened out, at least insofar as not wasting time in conducting lineups was concerned and scrapping the entire prosecution of a case by his action.

What could the D.A. tell the victim?

Clyde got to serve his profession in the interests of justice...not because of a mere technicality, as popular misunderstanding might have it. Rather, this was the everyday, real-life justice of trying to keep a monolithic government power machine fair and honest, making it functionally comply with inalienable principles of due process for all and always. It was a small step in the process of seeking what tempering mercy is possible, leaving some hopeful opportunity for rehabilitation instead of self-perpetuating recidivism, and, in short, making the adversarial system of jurisprudence actually work rather than letting it default into raw inquisitorial despotism.

10

Fast Food - Dial 911

Gabriella was a strong person, the tough product of a tough life. She knew how to use a gun and had the guts to kill if she needed to. She had been a drug moll for a long time, with one U. S. Federal drug felony conviction on her record, having been caught in a criminal conspiracy case in Mexicali.

By the time Gabriella was 32, she was the mother of three children, ages 9, 7, and 2. She was trying to make a better life by studying to become a hairdresser. However, she needed support and was still living with a major drug dealer who trafficked cocaine over the border from Mexico.

Gabriella's boyfriend and his partner were in the business of importing bananas...rotten bananas. Rotten bananas interfered with the ability of the dogs at the border to sniff out the drugs, which were the principal product of their import business. It worked...they went undetected.

Somehow the partners had a falling out. As so often happens when banana importers have a falling-out, Gabriella's guy ended up as a sole proprietor. The killing of the odd man out occurred in a little border town in San Diego County, which was sort of policed by the sheriff's department…the crime was never solved.

Her boyfriend was frequently away on business, sometimes for weeks. Gabriella's attendance at beauty school required her to be away from home eight hours a day. When she left the children each morning, she locked the doors carefully and the three children stayed inside alone. The nine-year-old boy had to take care of the two younger kids. The seven-year-old had health and mental problems, but also helped care for the two-year-old, who was still in diapers.

While Gabriella was at school one day, her kids got hungry. They decided the thing to do was Dial 911 like it said on television. They did this, and ordered fast food hamburgers. The Emergency Services operator soon determined the youngsters were alone and without adult supervision. The call was referred to the police department's Child Protective Service. The telephone call was traced and two Child Protective officers, with two uniformed cops, were soon at Gabriella's home.

The house was a simple, three-bedroom, one-bath place with an attached garage…nothing out of the ordinary…nothing suspicious…nothing unusual to suggest suspicious activities. Yet, after collecting the children in the front room, the officers decided to search the house. Of course, they had no search warrant and legally needed nothing else in the premises, since they had already secured the children's safety, which was the emergency purpose for which they had entered. In fact, the child protective personnel were already taking the kids away for safekeeping, in accordance with their standard operating procedures.

There was no emergency or dangerous situation when the other cops undertook a detailed search of the house. Obviously, no children could be hiding in the kitchen drawers, but they looked there anyway and found automatic weapons and bullets. This was blood in the water to the sharks of law enforcement.

The Federal Bureau of Alcohol, Tobacco, and Firearms was brought in to conduct a more thorough investigation. A further search by these professionals uncovered a cache of automatic weapons, sawed-off shotguns, and other blatantly illegal weaponry and ammunition. At first they thought they had intercepted a Mexican expeditionary force preparing to re-take the State of California, but then they discovered in the bedroom closets, instead of military uniforms, neatly stacked bundles of cocaine...more than 300 kilos of cocaine.

This required intervention of the Federal Drug Enforcement Agency. During their search, they found more neatly stacked bundles...52 pounds of United States currency. They weighed it, because it would have taken too long to count.

This discovery, of course, required the assistance of the Federal Treasury Department, Criminal Investigation Division of the Internal Revenue Service. They secured the money to make sure it was safe...you bet...they weren't taking any chances!
They probably thought about calling the President himself, but must have figured he'd be too busy playing golf and wouldn't want to be disturbed.

These search, seizure and secure operations took several hours. Early on, they called the Deputy District Attorney, who was assigned to coordinate with the U.S. Attorney's office. He was an earnest, honest, dull, young man who had been plodding through the District Attorney's bureaucracy for the past eight years. Everything had already been located when he arrived, and he could not believe his eyes; he had never been at a crime scene with such quantities of weapons, drugs, and cash all together in the same place at the same time. He was dumbfounded! In his state of disbelief, he never thought to question the propriety of the six-hour, warrantless search by the various agencies.

Late in the afternoon upon her return from beauty school, Gabriella found a fleet of police vehicles at her house and her home filled with cops. Some were even on her roof with metal detectors. She didn't know her children were gone, but understood she was in big, big trouble. Not knowing what to do, she stayed away and went to wait at a neighbor's house.

Around 7:00 p.m....eight hours after the original 911 call...six hours after the arrival of the Deputy D.A., someone asked the Assistant District Attorney about the specific authority for the search, "Where's the warrant?" Reportedly, he turned as red as a road flare, realizing that every agency that had made the search assumed that the previous agency had done the paperwork.

Of course, the first officers on the scene had been from the child protective service, which operated as if everything they ever did was an emergency. They *never* bothered with warrants. But they hadn't needed to search in order to protect and save the children. With all of the unforeseen activity, no one bothered to find out if the children ever got anything to eat!

So, since no exigent circumstances had prevented obtaining a warrant, all the searches were *fruit of the poisonous tree* and none of the weapons, drugs, or money seized could ever be used as evidence.

By eight o' clock that night, although the house was still crowded with officers and lit up with portable lights like a movie set, Gabriella finally could wait no longer to find out about her children. When she went to her home and asked about them, she was immediately placed under arrest and taken to the Metropolitan Correctional Center in San Diego. She was told nothing about her children. That was the kind of omission the authorities used to inflict cruel and unusual punishment...even before trial.

Gabriella was charged with conspiracy to transport drugs, possession of illegal weapons, income tax evasion, and child endangerment. Next day, the newspapers reported that Gabriella, with a prior conviction for drug trafficking, was facing a $1,100,000.00 fine and 35 years in prison. Someone at the M.C.C. got her to call a good attorney...Clyde!

After meeting with Gabriella at the Federal lockup, Clyde immediately secured her release on bail because she had three children to care for. Then he had the children released to her since, if they had ever been in danger, nothing dangerous remained in their home...everything having been seized by all the various agencies.

With his client reunited with her children, Clyde got on with the case itself. He was able to convince the authorities that the weapons, drugs and money did not belong to Gabriella, but to her banana-importing roommate-boyfriend. He, out of an abundance of caution, had disappeared, apparently having been tipped off by someone in the neighborhood when the raid happened. But when his identity became known, the Sheriff's homicide unit made the connection to his murdered former banana-importing business partner.

They wanted to charge Gabriella with conspiracy in the murder along with everything else. Clyde quickly acted to quash that ambition, demonstrating there was no evidence that Gabriella even knew the deceased. That wasn't important to the authorities though...all they wanted was someone to prosecute, and they couldn't find the obvious suspect...the banana entrepreneur-boyfriend. But they did have Gabriella, so they came after her full-bore and loaded for bear. Her bail was revoked and she was incarcerated once again in the M.C.C.

For a while, it looked like the Deputy D.A., who by then, had one foot in the Office of the U.S. Attorney, would be prosecuting both the State and Federal side of the criminal charges. This jurisdictional crossover was unprecedented, and Clyde's nose for smoke and fire became alerted.

Clyde subpoenaed the officers who had been at the scene in preparation for the upcoming hearings. Pursuant to the subpoenas, Clyde's investigator began interviewing those who would be testifying. It soon became clear that none of them had obtained a warrant, all of them saying the officers arriving before them must have done so. It was like a game of Ring Around the Rosie...everyone dancing around in a circle...one guy pointing to the next guy, who was pointing to the next guy, who was pointing to....well, you get the picture. Eventually they all fell down!

At this point, the Government gave the Deputy D.A. some help...first one, then two, then three additional prosecutors. Whenever Clyde visited the Deputy D.A., another of the prosecutors was always present as a sort of mentor. Clearly, the young prosecutor was the key weak link in the Government's long chain of abundant evidence. The whole crowd of prosecutors could not obscure the fact that the Deputy D.A. had been at a major crime scene for six hours and had never sought to obtain a search warrant. This kind of mistake is a career-ending failure, but he and his backup team just put a confident, aggressive face on their posture, blithely breezing along, whistling in the dark graveyard of their fundamental debacle, hoping beyond hope that something...anything...would happen to make the whole predicament go away.

Their main obstacle was Clyde...he was not going away...neither was the Government's catastrophe. Clyde prepared a subpoena which was served on the Deputy D.A. to testify. It is more than rare for a prosecutor to have to testify as a defense witness in the case he's prosecuting, and this was newsworthy. The newspapers were about to make a field day of the incompetence in the Office of the District Attorney and the Office of the U. S. Attorney.

After the subpoena was served on the prosecutor and the hearing was scheduled, Clyde's office got a call from a very senior Assistant U. S. Attorney requesting a face-to-face discussion of the case. Clyde went alone and was not escorted to the Assistant U. S. Attorney's office, but to a separate private room. This particular attorney had previously quit the Office of the U. S. Attorney after refusing to bend a rule at the request of a Federal Judge. He was eventually reinstated and maintained his reputation for honesty, forthrightness, integrity, and thoroughness. He and Clyde held one another in mutual respect.

He didn't play games...he got right to the point. To avoid further embarrassment of the government and public exposure of the Assistant District Attorney's total incompetence, he offered a deal whereby Gabriella could plead to a felony; she would be given credit for the 139 days she spent in custody, suspension of the balance of a minimum sentence and no fine. He agreed that there would be no repercussions from her violation of probation from her prior felony conviction. She was reunited with her children without intervention of Child Protective Services, and she would be allowed to remain in the United States without threat of deportation.

Here, justice prevailed.

11

The Dirty Lawyer

Gary had led a privileged life. His father was a well-to-do banker, who for many years was the senior vice president of a major bank. They lived in a comfortable residential community, where his mother was an educator who had risen to the head of the entire school board.

Gary never had to worry about much, but didn't leave well enough alone. Somewhere along the line, he heard there was a great profit in cocaine. He began his career in high school, developing connections which would ultimately lead him to a Colombian cartel networking throughout Southern California. He catapulted himself to success, as drug dealers are prone to do, but made the same mistake so many others had made...he began using cocaine himself.

With the use of cocaine, particularly when it is free or nearly free, excess is inevitable. Excess usage quickly leads to paranoia. So it did with Gary. He began exhibiting irate and erratic behavior, which did not go unnoticed by his drug-dealing underlings. Some of them were disgruntled and decided to take Gary down, push him out and take over. Knowing death could easily follow such ambitions, they decided to hide behind a weakling dupe, allowing that patsy to think he could move into Gary's position if he became the informant who snitched to the narcs about Gary.

By this time, Gary's drug dealing involved two motorcycle gangs and distribution centers, which included churches and some lawyers' offices. Ralph, one of those lawyers had been infamous as a no-deal, hell-for-leather, out-for-blood prosecutor when he was with the District Attorney's Office, and later notoriously successful as an unscrupulous defense attorney. However, he had his own nemesis. He was a compulsive gambler and frequently closed up his law office in the evening, and then drove to Los Angeles to gamble all night in the card rooms in the pre-Indian casino days. Then Ralph would drive back in the morning just in time for court…no sleep…just pills.

Of course, this regimen inevitably undermined Ralph's base mettle and he began to make looser and looser decisions. He would receive cocaine from Gary and arrange for it to be picked up by other so called clients, who were mostly members of motorcycle gangs.

One of the outlaw bikers who regularly visited his office was a charmer nick-named Snake. Ralph always saw how much blow Snake had been entrusted to deliver. Snake, of course, dutifully delivered the goods. But one time Snake shorted the load and got himself suddenly dead. Homicide detectives don't spend a lot of time worrying about snuffed biker druggies, but they did discover that Snake, Ralph, and Gary had all been busily engaged with one another in what appeared to be an unsavory relationship.

It was just a matter of time before things fell apart for Gary. A search warrant executed on his home turned up a substantial amount of cash. Although, like many drug dealers, he had two safes, the cops immediately zeroed in on the one which held the money…a sure sign of a tip-off. Gary thought he knew who set him up.

Ralph, who normally would have defended Gary, felt the matter was too close to home and instead gave Gary's case to Clyde Munsell. However, wishing to keep a close eye on things, Ralph decided to defend Gary's wife, who was a co-defendant in the State criminal case.

After only a brief meeting, Clyde knew Gary needed treatment at a primary care facility and got him admitted to an upscale private hospital which was one of the area's best recovery centers. After just a few days, Gary realized the jig was up and made two calls, both using the public telephone. First, through a series of calls to Colombia he sold his cocaine ring to a cartel. Second, and even more stupid, he put out a murder-for-hire contract on the guy he suspected was the informant.

Unfortunately, the narcotics officers on his case had wiretap orders on the pay phones at the recovery center. As a consequence, Gary was indicted by the Federal Grand Jury for narcotics trafficking and conspiracy to distribute a dangerous drug...both Federal felonies. Fortunately, the bullets aimed at the informant only ripped out his stomach without killing him, so Gary did not get charged with murder...only conspiracy to commit it. So, the one big problem Gary had before he entered the recovery center had ballooned to three big problems before he got out. He not only had the original State narcotics charges, now he also faced Federal narcotics charges and a conspiracy rap involving the attempted murder of the informant. It looked like Gary was going away for a very long time.

Following his arrest for the original drug case, Gary had been out on bail to allow his treatment at the recovery center. The new charges brought new arrest and custody problems but also some new opportunities. Clyde decided the best thing to do was to pit the Federal system against the State system...the two rarely work together, contrary to popular fiction. As the Assistant D.A. got ready to pick up Gary at one of the State Court hearings, Clyde deposited Gary in Federal protective custody pursuant to a writ *ad testificandum, as* a potential cooperating witness in the Federal case. This made Gary ineligible for bail and unavailable for any State Court hearings.

Gary was aware he was looking at a life sentence in prison and began to take stock of his situation. He could no longer believe he would somehow walk free. He also woke up to the fact that the incarceration of his wife would be used by the prosecution as leverage to help him roll over defenselessly.

About this time, one of the narcotics agents leaked to Clyde that they were really after the dirty lawyer. Clyde knew that Gary's first lawyer, Lucas, a denizen of the Orange County

Riviera, was a longtime outspoken proponent of marijuana who also had a reputation for trafficking in weed. The narcotics agents schemed to lead Clyde to believe that it was Lucas they had originally targeted. Sharing this information with Gary, Clyde saw that Gary had no love for his former lawyer and immediately agreed to give him up.

The Assistant D.A. handling the original State case was a consummate professional who was soon to be elevated to a judgeship. He agreed that Gary's testimony to convict a dirty lawyer was more important than getting Gary himself and agreed to recommend a probationary sentence for Gary in the State case. He also agreed to dismiss the charges against Gary's wife. With no case against her, she would no longer require a lawyer and could drop Ralph.

As these events were developing, bigger revelations were awaiting. Gary was still in Federal protective custody but, chained and with a guard, was allowed to accompany Clyde to a readiness conference held in State Court. Gary's wife and her attorney, Ralph were seated next to them. In a conversation between the four of them, the fact that the Feds really wanted the *dirty lawyer* was broached. In shocked alarm, Ralph blurted out, *"That's me! It's me they want?"*

This happened in the spectator section of one of the very small courtrooms used for hearings, not one of the big rooms used for jury-trials. The entire court heard Ralph's panicky outburst. Clyde quickly got the four of them, along with Gary's guard, out into the hallway. Clyde took Ralph aside and learned the whole story involving Gary, Ralph, and the late Snake, because of whose murder Gary's problems might include capital charges, after all.

There are times when the best attack is to retreat. Clyde immediately put the court hearing on continuance and proceeded to do three things to shore up the defense position. First, he had Gary returned to protective custody. Second, he told Ralph to get himself a lawyer. Third, he got a new lawyer for Gary. He hired a man who not only had no strong ties to Ralph, but was also the former boss of the Federal prosecutor on Gary's case.

Continuing to manipulate the situation, Clyde then got a deal whereby Gary would agree to testify against Ralph in return for probationary sentences in all his Federal cases; the conspiracy case involving the near-fatal shooting of the suspected informant would be dismissed.

Ralph would probably have asked Clyde to be his defense lawyer, but Clyde now had a conflict of interest which relieved him not only of representing Ralph, but also of continuing his representation of Gary.

Ralph retained Mike, a glad-handing, sweaty-palmed attorney of Irish persuasion, whom Clyde had previously met when he personally took him to an Alcoholics Anonymous meeting. Clyde explained Ralph's case to Mike and laid out his defense plan.

Clyde paid numerous visits to the Assistant U.S. Attorney handling the Federal prosecution of Ralph, laying out facts as necessary during those meetings. Clyde was present when the revelation hit the Assistant U.S. Attorney that he had enough on Ralph to charge him under the RICO statutes which could result in a sentence of five years to life. Since this was all under the pre-sentencing guidelines of 1988, that meant a substantial amount of time behind the walls. Instead, Clyde quick-stepped and suggested two counts of a lesser included offense, which would result in a maximum sentence of five years. He shared this with Mike. Everyone was in agreement.

Gary and his nominal lawyer took the plea deal for probationary sentences and dismissal of the assault case which Clyde had engineered before stepping out of the case. The case against Gary's wife was dismissed by special appearance which did not require the appearance of an attorney.

Mike, looking on in bewilderment as all this surged over his head, just stood with Ralph and gawked in awe as three lifetime sentences disappeared from the grasp of the District Attorney and the U.S. Attorney.

Lucas, the pot-promoting dirty lawyer of Orange County the agents sought to use as a lure was not touched in this go-round; the D.E.A. decided to save him for another day.

Ralph served only seventeen months of his sentence, over-came his gambling problem and was rehabilitated to once again be licensed to practice law. His nominal lawyer, Mike, remained as vapid as ever and probably still has sweaty palms.

Gary was released after one year in protective custody in

the M.C.C., the Federal high-rise lock-up in downtown San Diego. Today he is a recovered addict and an upstanding and respected real estate broker.

12

The Gold Rolex Mine

Richard Wangler was an enterprising fellow who believed he could create a tax-free entity and by doing so avoid paying income tax. He formed The Native American Indian Nations Foundation, Inc. Wangler filed for his 501(c)3 charity status. Tax exempt status for charitable purposes is readily available. However, Richard's philanthropic endeavors were never intended to benefit any Indians. The money he raised was destined instead to benefit the ultimate beneficiary...Richard himself.

Once he had the tax exempt status in hand, the Foundation *discovered* a gold mine in the Tehachapi Mountains of California, amidst an area of geological conglomerate. Gold occurs in specific geological formations throughout the world, but never in conglomerate. This did not give pause to Richard, who wasn't interested in the gold in the hills, but in the gold from his investors.

Richard employed salesmen from Sweden to sell interests in the gold mining ventures. The checks he collected went into the corporate account of the Foundation and were transferred by wire to the Republic of Vanuatu, formerly the New Hebrides island group in the South Pacific. The day after the wire hit the bank in Vanuatu, a like amount was immediately wired back to Richard's other Foundation account in California. The moment the funds were cleared, he emptied that account and *donated* the funds for his personal pleasures and enrichment.

Initially, this raised no eyebrows in the Government. However, after Richard had washed several million dollars in this manner, the Government noticed the Form 990 tax exempt organization tax returns did not jibe with the bank accounts. Richard maintained this did not matter since all the money was being used for charitable purposes.

In the course of income tax fraud prosecution, the Government starts almost always with a civil audit. If criminality is found, the civil division of the Internal Revenue Service, Department of Treasury postpones their work and refers the matter to the criminal division of the IRS. That is what happened with Richard.

Our Government believes the 92 regional offices of the United States Attorney throughout our country know nothing about taxes or accounting. Consequently, every criminal tax fraud indictment results in the dispatch of a special prosecutor from Washington, D.C. to the jurisdiction where the case will be tried. The special prosecutor is generally not admitted to practice law in the state where the indictment was issued and must therefore work with an Assistant United States Attorney who is admitted to the bar in the state where the prosecution takes place. This double-teaming is universal in all tax fraud cases.

Richard inherited an erstwhile aggressive prosecutor named Martin Dorset from somewhere back East. Mr. Dorset flew out happily to sunny southern California whenever the occasion arose.

Wangler was referred to Clyde by an attorney who was a mutual acquaintance. He knew something of Richard's Indian Nations Foundation and had been to the corporate offices where he noticed that the decor included Indian rugs and some supposed Indian artifacts. Knowing nothing about taxes himself, he referred the case to Clyde.

Clyde's first aim was to determine whether or not a violation occurred in the Grand Jury room. If, for instance, at any point in the Grand Jury proceedings an unauthorized person was admitted, the indictment could be dismissed upon motion. Clyde quickly learned that Mr. Dorset was not a member of the State Bar of California but indeed had been in the Grand Jury room. It was too juicy a morsel for him to miss. To secure the indictment, Mr. Dorset actually presented the case to the Federal Grand Jury. Luckily for the Government, Mr. Dorset had been accompanied by the Assistant United States Attorney assigned to the case who was admitted to practice in California. He was a righteous fellow who did not mind Mr. Dorset's overwhelming ego and one-upmanship. A single line in the Grand Jury transcript reflected the presence of the local U.S. Attorney during Mr. Dorset's presentation. But for this, Clyde could have won a dismissal.

As the case proceeded, accounting records from the several banks were produced. Even a fool could see the exact amounts down to the last penny were being routinely wired back from Vanuatu a day or two after they had been deposited in the overseas account of Richard's *charitable* corporation. The total sum of all of those deposits found their way back to Southern California and ultimately disappeared with no expenditures for any discernable charitable purpose. As the Government's case grew, Clyde worked with both the special prosecutor and the local Assistant U.S. Attorney with whom Clyde had worked many times before, trying to find a chink in the armor. Clyde began seeing them so often they quit appearing as a pair. This was their mistake.

Clyde noticed there was something about Mr. Dorset that didn't equate with the image Clyde had observed in other special prosecutors, who felt that somehow they were better than the attorneys in the local office since they worked out of the nation's Capital. Mr. Dorset usually dressed conservatively in a blue suit and a two-tone tie. However, Mr. Dorset wore a $10,000.00 gold Rolex watch on his left wrist, which he was in the habit of flashing during any meetings with Clyde.

Clyde realized Mr. Dorset's flashy-gold-Rolex ego could be mined to Richard Wangler's benefit. The judge in the case, before whom Clyde had appeared many times, was a strict, no-

nonsense fellow elevated from the defense bar, a rarity in the system where the majority of the judges had formerly been *prosecutors.* The judge knew what was what when defense lawyers were doing their thing. Clyde knew he must be careful not to irk the judge or his plan might backfire.

Eventually it became evident to Clyde that a plea of some sort would be necessary if Mr. Wangler was not to disappear for a very long time. Clyde found a rather innocuous count in the indictment which would assure that Mr. Wangler would serve less than a year if found guilty. He approached Mr. Dorset, in the absence of the local Assistant U.S. Attorney, with an offer to have Richard plead guilty on that count. Clyde knew the Assistant U.S. Attorney would be okay with anything to which Mr. Dorset had agreed.

Considering Richard owed over $350,000.00 in taxes, this was not a bad disposition. Moreover, the year would be done at a country-club Federal lockup which housed white-collar felons so tame the facility used female guards. Even the food at this institution had a favorable reputation.

Clyde's plan was to reiterate every part of the plea bargain to Mr. Dorset on the record before the judge. In this manner, it would tie the hands of the Government, as well as the defendant, for future proceedings. The trick was that Mr. Dorset, who probably had little trial experience and was glad to have the case pled out to avoid a trial, agreed that the plea bargain would encompass all tax ramifications and no taxes would be due. This was very satisfying to Clyde, since no one had received a deal that sweet since President Richard Nixon, who backdated the charitable deduction of his memoirs using a typewriter that hadn't been made when the documents were supposedly prepared.

After the civil division of the IRS suspends their investigation of the taxpayer, they forward it to the criminal division. Once the criminal division has concluded the prosecution, they normally refer the matter back to the civil division to collect the taxes, penalties and interest. In Mr. Wangler's case, however, Clyde's plea bargain resulted in civil tax immunity of manifestly Presidential quality.

At the plea proceeding, Clyde reiterated, sentence by sentence, the entirety of the deal into the court record, being careful to stop at the end of each sentence and turn to Mr. Dorset to ask: "Is that correct? Is that the Government's position?" Mr. Dorset, gold Rolex and ego flashing, was able to speak as the voice of the United States Government 52 times, affirming the plea bargain. It was a complex, prolonged procedure, and the judge failed to realize that the Government was giving away the tax collection farm.

After the plea deal, Clyde accompanied Richard to the probation department, as he always did with his clients. Mr. Dorset's light bulb finally lit when he had sudden realization that all was not as he had hoped. He caught up with Clyde and Richard at the elevator, frantically complaining, *"Something's wrong! Something's wrong! I misspoke, we have to go back to court!"* Clyde replied, "Unfortunately, Mr. Dorset, the matter is off calendar now...the case is over!" My last question to you on the record was, "Are we adjourned?" You're response on the record was, "Yes, we are." As the elevator prepared to take Clyde and his client away, the thunderstruck expression on Mr. Dorset's face was eclipsed by the closing elevator doors.

Some months later, although the Government tried to get out of the deal, Clyde would not budge. Ultimately, Mr. Wangler got eleven months in the desert prison spa and all his ill-gotten gains tax free. Of course, the client was not satisfied with this, thinking he should have received probation instead of jail time for his huge, unarguably, deliberate fraud. Clyde told Richard he would trade...Richard could give Clyde the $1,100,000 plunder and Clyde would do the 11 months.

The client was actually out in eight months, with a fortune and a tan. However, he resentfully refused to pay Clyde more money to continue his representation when the Government pressured him after his release. So, he tried to represent himself. Of course, he didn't know any more about enforcing the plea bargain than he did about Indians, so the Government broke the deal and hit him with the taxes, interest, and civil penalties...he should have stuck with Clyde.

13

The Missing Admonishment

Angelo was two months old when his mother and older sisters left his gangster father in Italy and moved to America, where he grew up amid hard-working, law-abiding relatives who operated a successful restaurant business. His mother, then his sisters, became U.S. citizens. But Angelo's mother was afraid to lose her only son to the military draft, so she did not arrange citizenship for him and he remained a resident alien.

All was good until Angelo contracted a disease so rare only one hundred people in the entire world had it. It was incurable but treatable by a medication chemically similar to the illegal drug methamphetamine, commonly referred to as *speed*. When he was still in his early twenties, Angelo discovered after experimenting with the drug that speed controlled his disease as well or better than the medicine prescribed by the doctors. By taking meth, he could feel…*normal*.

Like most speed users, Angelo eventually came to the

conclusion that it made sound economic sense to deal in the drug, so his own daily dosage was free rather than costly.

Over 95% of all contemporary drug enforcement cases originate from an informant. The drug enforcement branch of the criminal justice system is hooked on, and organized to exploit this phenomenon. Their interactive network for processing snitch information about drug trafficking is mapped out as thoroughly as a Rand McNally Street Guide. There are major routes marked out for big-time cartel dealers and minor side streets for small-time amateur dealers. Everything is charted, indexed and cross-referenced.

As a small-time operator, Angelo flew under the radar until one of his dealer confederates was arrested. This is a commonplace, inevitable scenario in the trade; every dealer, however minor, knows another who gets busted.

The Drug Enforcement Administration is not lazy, but it is overwhelmingly busy. While it takes a lot of time and effort for them to hook and reel in the big fish, they can cook a lot of small fries...simple productivity. One dealer is caught and gets off lightly if he snitches and arranges for two more to get snagged; if those two help themselves by helping to net two more apiece, the DEA soon has scored a catch of seven. Do the math: multiplication builds big bureaucratic statistics.

Angelo got nailed just after the Federal Government had yet again reformed its sentencing rules. With this change came mandatory minimum sentences, which for conspiracy to distribute methamphetamine, as in Angelo's case, was ten years.

Angelo's defense lawyer for that case arranged for a plea agreement whereby the ten years would be suspended if he cooperated with the Government by snitching. As in all cases with the Feds at that time, the plea agreement was put in writing, including caveats that if the defendant got arrested again during the case for a like crime, lied to the Government, or otherwise breached the agreement, he automatically had to serve the full term of suspended sentence.

Angelo may have entered into the plea agreement in good faith, but his attorney at that time was less virtuous, being himself meantime indicted for cocaine distribution. So, Angelo got a second lawyer...then that protector of legal rights got charged with pimping and pandering. Angelo had to get a third defense lawyer, who was also a drug addict and suddenly went missing, much later to surface, brain-fried, in a South American country. Now, Angelo had to get a fourth attorney, who was merely going bankrupt due to severe financial abuses, and soon disappeared with as much of Angelo's retainer and his other clients' funds as he could embezzle from his trust account. He was disbarred; his whereabouts yet unknown. Finally, Angelo needed a fifth lawyer

During the several years of lawyer flops, Angelo was floundering in the System, being worked endlessly by his controlling DEA agents to set up other dealers for arrest. No one in the meth business had yet learned that good ol' popular young Angelo had been busted, so he remained a viable snitch. Eventually, Angelo got tired of being exploited by bad lawyers and insatiable DEA puppeteers alike, decided he had done his fair share of snitching and figured he could escape the whole treadmill by simply tipping off his dealer friends not to say anything incriminating when he came around wired with a DEA microphone.

Of course, Angelo's new idea was old news to the DEA...they'd seen it all before. After a couple of idle chit-chat conversations with targeted dealers when Angelo was wired, they marked him for a traitor. So the DEA set its own trap, arresting one of the targeted dealers Angelo had warned on unrelated charges. He promptly made a deal on his charges by turning reverse snitch, admitting Angelo had warned him about being wired.

That was enough for the Feds. They revoked the plea bargain arrangement with Angelo...off he went to serve the ten years. This all happened at an unusual time in national legal developments. Angelo's actual court appearance wherein he entered into his plea occurred in early 1989, less than six months after the new Federal sentencing guidelines went into effect but three years before the Immigration and Naturalization Service (INS) decided everyone in Angelo's category, i.e., non-citizens with Federal drug convictions, would never be eligible to remain in the United States.

In such a case involving a non-citizen, the standard practice was for an admonition to be made in the written plea bargain agreement itself, which notifies the defendant that if the court accepts the plea and allows the defendant to work as a cooperating informant for the Feds rather than going to prison, the defendant would still be subject to deportation after the agreement was over. However, this was not the standard practice in 1989, so no such admonition was included in Angelo's plea agreement.

Angelo began serving his ten year term in 1991 and was a model prisoner, participating in voluntary drug recovery and rehabilitation programs, and maintaining his health by managing his rare medical condition with proper prescription medication.

In 1992, the INS changed some of its "administrative" policies and procedures. These particular changes involved interpretation and application of the law, but since they were made at the bureaucratic level they were considered *administrative,* like janitorial maintenance procedures, and were applied to all INS cases, whether or not the case pre-existed the changes. They acted as if their interpretation and application of the law were exempt from the *ex post facto* restrictions of the United States Constitution. The INS decided any non-citizen with a Federal drug conviction would be deported to their native country, regardless of plea bargain and without regard to admonishment or any further complications such as due process. To young Angelo, this meant he would be sent back to the country he left when he was two months old, even though he knew no one there and was unable able to speak the native language.

The Government was sued by Angelo in 1992 when he asked the obvious questions about remaining in the United States, but received no acceptable answers. However, since the INS doesn't act like normal branches of the Government, they didn't do anything in response to the suit. Rather, they just passed it along and waited. Several months before Angelo was to be released after serving his ten-year sentence minus one year for his drug rehab class, he was informed that the INS had now awakened and decided to deport him. He would be deported on the day he was released from his prison sentence.

To insure there was no gap between the time of his release and the moment of his departure, one month before his release from Federal prison he was spirited off to an INS detention facility so his exodus would be facilitated and his ticket would be one way, paid for by the very Government that had kept him incarcerated for the last nine years. To further confuse the issue, the Government, while releasing him from Federal prison in California, did not ship him to Los Angeles for deportation, but rather shipped him to Louisiana, farther away from family and friends who might help him.

At about this time, Angelo's family got together and decided they had had enough of the bad lawyer syndrome and needed to get a new reliable lawyer for Angelo. They sought the advice of an acquaintance who was an administrative law judge of Italian heritage. The judge knew Clyde from their mutual involvements in San Diego's Little Italy business and cultural community. Clyde became Angelo's fifth lawyer. He looked at the case, got all the documents from the four clowns that preceded him, and made some evaluations. The glaring lack of the admonishment in the original plea agreement, both the written form and the court transcript, made clear that neither the Government nor the court warned Angelo he would be deported regardless.

Clyde first began his work by arranging for Angelo's bail. The INS doesn't grant bail unless ordered by the deportation court. Clyde hired the best deportation lawyer in the vicinity of the INS facility in Louisiana. Being local, he knew the ropes and which ones to pull. The bail process was a bureaucratic obstacle course of hoops and hurdles, but Clyde came out the other end with Angelo out of custody and a subsequent hearing scheduled which allowed Clyde some maneuvering time.

When Clyde first brought the missing admonishment to the Government's attention, they turned a blind eye to the entire situation and ignored his argument. They were unwilling to change Angelo's plea bargain agreement to allow him at least the opportunity to avoid deportation. After several hearings before the INS judge, Clyde made no progress. So he hired the immigration lawyer who had been the former law partner of the INS judge. This kept matters moving and Angelo's bail in place, but it became obvious the INS establishment was obliviously disinterested in considering its problems vis-à-vis the essential Constitutional legal issues involved. The Government was in stonewalling denial mode; no one in the Office of the U. S.

Attorney or the INS was going to take any professional risk to acknowledge the emperor had no clothes.

Finally there was nothing left but to take the matter to the Court of Appeals. Clyde made it clear to the Government that if they only let Angelo stay in America, the whole issue would go away, but that if the appeal was upheld, it would impact innumerable cases of foreign drug convicts. But there was no one on the Government side who dared admit they had been wrong all along, so they could not take the easy way out.

Three years later, the Court of Appeals unanimously decided in Angelo's favor. The case was published and became a precedent. As a result, over 22,000 deported alien drug dealers became eligible to return to the U.S.A.

Meanwhile, Angelo had been working multiple jobs to support his young family and pay his income tax to support the Government and its agencies which routinely ignored the United States Constitution. He continued to live the American dream. Unfortunately, so did the 22,000 alien drug dealers.

14
The Crime of Art

While working in the investment banking industry in New York City, Rex developed a fancy for art auctions. He and his boyfriend, Duke, began to frequent the auctions at the two richest and most famous auction houses in New York. They began to observe other familiar faces of those who frequented the auctions and were soon able to identify the celebrated dealers of the glamorous New York art world. They also noticed certain individuals who always seemed to attend the auctions, but were unknown, non-entities who were not among the recognized personalities of the gallery culture. Having become devoted fans of the whole Big Apple art scene, Rex and Duke's curiosity was piqued by the identity of those mysterious habitués. With a bit of back-channel nosing around, they discovered that they were shills for the auction houses; used to boost the bids for certain items or stifle bidding on others being offered for sale.

In those days, Sotheby's and Christie's were clandestinely involved in a world-sized price fixing scheme whereby they could control prices in the art-market and buy for their own inventories at undervalued prices. The scheme did not become public knowledge until about ten years after Rex and Duke discovered what was happening. Since the secrecy of the scheme was still so successfully maintained when the boys discovered it, they decided to seek ways and means to cash in on the illegal activity and steal a little for themselves.

They learned the telephone bidders at auctions were always anonymous. They were assigned a bidder number by a telephone clerk on the floor and could remain unknown to the auction house. The bidding process was arranged without ever meeting face-to-face with any house representatives.

Rex and Duke established numerous telephone bidding accounts at both auction houses, using fictitious identities and *borrowed* addresses. They rented a storefront in a nearly vacant building in Brooklyn and purchased second-hand printing equipment from a second-hand office supply company. Using a signature-printing block so their real signatures would not appear, they began printing phony cashier's checks. They established a *bank* with a prudential sounding name, using a mail drop service in Beverly Hills, California as the bank's address. Then as with any major financial institution, they installed a state-of-the-art telephone answering system that always answered on the second ring and always gave a busy signal on any given extension. Calls were never connected to a human being and always ending up taking a recorded message.

Being realistic schemers, they realized that any scam like the one they were perpetrating might very well lead to their getting caught. Creating yet another fictitious person and using real money orders, they rented a secure warehouse in another part of town to stash one-third of all of the booty they acquired as a *rainy day umbrella*.

Utilizing their numerous telephone bidding accounts at Sotheby's and Christie's, they began acquiring solid gold watches and other gold jewelry, which could easily be turned into cash. They directed that the purchases be delivered C.O.D. by UPS to one or more of the addresses they had *borrowed* for the respective fictitious buyers. The key element in these capers was the reliability of Big Brown's delivery service and the ability to track the shipments.

Based on the scheduled delivery date and time, the boys would stake out the *borrowed* delivery address. When the UPS truck arrived, Rex or Duke, nattily attired, would stride up to the driver outside of the house they had *borrowed*, and in a very businesslike manner say, "That package is probably for me." And give the driver the name of the fictitious buyer. Naturally, the busy driver would asked Mr. *Fictitious* to sign for the package and would accept one of the phony cashier's checks as payment., letting him take delivery right there on the sidewalk.

By the time the phony cashier's checks began to bounce, and the auction houses became aware of the scam, several hundred pieces of valuable jewelry had been stolen. Rex and Duke had turned two-thirds of the loot into cash by selling it in the black market, pawning it or trading pieces for legitimate goods. Using new phony names, they sold the legitimate goods they had acquired in auctions at the very same auction houses they had been swindling.

Not satisfied, they obtained some new check-printing equipment and established another specious bank. They then ran the same scam again for another few months. Ultimately, their simple little caper bagged several million dollars' worth of loot. But, since both of the victimized auction houses were so profitably engaged in their own illegal activities, they could afford to just write off their losses...for a while anyway. When cashier's checks from a second phony bank began to show up, and it appeared there was no end in sight, the Federal authorities were notified.

Normally, crimes against property do not have top priority and do not rate the expensive, labor-intensive law enforcement response accorded to crimes of violence involving guns, drugs and other such notorious violations. However, when notified by two important internationally acclaimed establishments like Sotheby's and Christie's, the authorities took notice and launched an all-out investigation.

Purchases and deliveries that fit the established pattern of the scam were staked out by the unprecedented procedure of having Federal agents in UPS brown clothes ride along on the Big Brown trucks. When Rex dipped into the well once too often, he was arrested as he exchanged a fraudulent bank check for a shipment of gold jewelry.

Rex's mother was the secretary to a major football coach who knew of Clyde. She retained him to defend her son. When Clyde visited Rex in jail, he had already been placed in protective isolation. Rex with his flaming frosted hair and face makeup did not exactly blend in with the general jail population. The warden feared that Rex might be forced against his will to become intimate friends with the other inmates. He was quickly released on bail.

Rex displayed no remorse for his crime. In fact he had been very resourceful in his judicious decision to keep one-third of the loot intact and readily available as his ante into the pot when it came time to play his hand in the legal system game. Not only did he advise Clyde about the stored loot, but he related the details of the scam being operated by the two auction houses.

They agreed that they would only reveal the first hole card...the intact booty that could be returned to the auction houses. Clyde brokered a deal to toss the million dollars' worth of jewelry into the pot in exchange for Rex's freedom. The auction houses and the authorities were glad to recover the loot and Rex got probation.

They never had to play their ace-in-the-hole...informing the authorities and the world about who and how the crime of art was being perpetrated by the rich and famous auctioneers. That crime continued unabated to pay big dividends until many years later when the whistle was blown by somebody else.

Sometimes, justice delayed is justice denied

15

Hot Coins

Dr. José B. Aguilar, immigrated to the United States and became licensed as a heart surgeon in 1976. He established a medical practice in the South Bay area of southern California where his bi-lingual capability would give him an advantage.

Despite having been educated in Spain, he was distrustful of the opportunities available in the Spanish system of socialized medicine and was disappointed by the lack of a recognized specialty in his chosen field of heart surgery.

His family was from a long line of Spanish royalty who were avid coin collectors. Their interests lay in coins from the medieval Visigoth period in Spain, which stretched from 760 to 1110 A.D. Coinage from that period depicted a substantial part of Spanish history. Dr. Aguilar, by virtue of his family's lineage and his personal dedication to the coin collection, was becoming a world-renowned specialist in coins from that period.

He and his brother, also a doctor, who had remained in Spain, had edited and published a Spanish book on medical terminology. Encouraged by the success of that endeavor, Dr. Aguilar decided to embark on yet another literary effort to publish a book about Spanish coins during the Visigoth period of medieval Spanish history. He acquired two publishers, both in Spain, who were highly enthusiastic about the project at first. But early on, it became clear that quality photographs would be essential for the book to become a literary or educational success.

In 1984, Dr. Aguilar realized that for his book to be all-encompassing, he would require assistance, not only from other collectors, but from the American Numismatic Society (ANS) in New York City. He began to borrow, on a temporary basis, coins from around the world from a host of other collectors. By 1989, these coins, when added to his own collection, amassed the world's most significant assemblage of more than two thousand Visigoth pieces, collectively valued at approximately $5,000,000.00.

He had joined the American Numismatic Society which maintained the world's largest coin collection (more than a million different examples). He quickly gained acceptance as a primary benefactor, having made annual donations to the Society of cash and antique coins averaging $100,000.00.

By November, 1988, Dr. Aguilar had established a working relationship with the hierarchy of the ANS, and had been assigned Dr. Bishop as his personal curator. However, as a result of the retirement of the ANS Museum director, Leslie Ellis and William Merchand, gained control of the museum.

Almost immediately, Dr. Aguilar felt the pinch. He was no longer afforded access to the museum with his camera equipment, nor was he permitted to remove coins for photographic purposes. He was relegated to humbly requesting copies of photographs through the staff of a newly-imposed and increasingly more difficult, red-tape bureaucracy. The resulting black and white photographs were of poor quality and unsuitable for use in his book.

Under increasing pressure from his Spanish publishers, Dr. Aguilar arrogantly concocted a plan to *borrow* the coins from the museum. He took them to his own photographic laboratory at his residence in California, photographed them with his highly specialized equipment and returned them on his next trip to the museum.

There had not been a physical inventory of all of the museum's coins since 1984. By 1988, however, three-quarters of the collection had been recorded in the museum's computer. The computerized inventory omitted two areas of the museum. The first area housed the Spanish coin collections and the second, the American Cent collection, an area of the museum never visited by Dr. Aguilar.

Dr. Aguilar enjoyed the unstated, but tacit approval of Dr. Bishop, his personal curator, to remove the coins from the museum and photograph them in his photo lab. There was no difficulty until February of 1989, when the museum personnel became aware of coins missing from the American Cent collection. They reported the loss to Chubb, their insurance carrier. Without notice to any of the Society's members or patrons, Chubb Insurance Company hired *Banacek-style* insurance investigators, Edward Reilly & Son, to investigate the loss.

Hidden cameras were installed in all areas of the museum. At first, the cameras recorded no evidence that was of any value to the investigation, but on April 1, 1989, Dr. Aguilar was filmed removing coins from the Spanish Visigoth collection. After Dr. Aguilar returned to California from New York, Dr. Bishop was conscripted into a plot to snare him.

A great deal of excitement was generated among the world's coin community by the announcement of a presentation dinner and dance in Dr. Aguilar's honor. A cornerstone bearing his name was to be laid at the ANS Museum building during the event scheduled on April 15, 1989.

Earlier on the day he and his entire family arrived in New York for the gala event, he once again visited the area of the museum which housed the Visigoth coin collection. He was ushered into the area by Dr. Bishop and a new assistant curator, whom he had never met.

By then he had completed more than two-thirds of his book which had grown to more than 700 pages. Dr. Aguilar selected 13 coins from the collection with the intention of photographing and later returning them. He spirited them from the museum and hid the coins in his room at the Harvard Club which had generously been arranged for his family by the museum.

Dr. Aguilar and his family had dressed for the dinner and were on their way down the sweeping staircase, when they were suddenly surrounded by agents from the Frauds Division of the New York City District Attorney's Office and the officers from NYPD. They had been alerted by the new *assistant curator* who was, in fact, an Edward Reilly & Son investigator. A crew from a local television station was there to televise the scandalous arrest. So shocked and mortified by the unexpected predicament, Dr. Aguilar fainted dead away on the spot and remained unconscious for several hours. His family was totally crushed and completely devastated when the search of their quarters uncovered the 13 missing coins.

Still suffering the effects of his blackout and before being advised of his right to counsel, the prosecution claimed Dr. Aguilar gave a highly incriminating videotaped interview at the police department, wherein he ill-advisedly likened his love for coins to that of a man's love of a mistress.

A consent search warrant was issued, as a result of which Dr. Aguilar's entire coin collection was seized from his private vault, his residence and his offices in San Diego, California. The 2,000 coins were assembled at the San Diego Police Department and in accordance with the language of the warrant. Arrangements were made for the coins to be returned to the magistrate in New York City who had executed the warrant.

Leslie Ellis and William Merchand arrived in San Diego to take possession of the coins, but in violation of the explicit language in the warrant, and with the full knowledge of the police department, took Dr. Aguilar's entire collection, not just the coins enumerated in the warrant. Interestingly, the Edward Reilly & Sons investigators, made a point of noting the break in the chain of custody when Ellis and Merchand left for New York with the coins.

By August 15, 1989, 83 missing coins, including the 13 coins borrowed by Dr. Aguilar, were recovered by the ANS Museum. The other improperly seized coins were not returned to Dr. Aguilar, but were held over his head like a hatchet until the criminal case against him resulted in an unfavorable disposition.

After his release from custody he returned to San Diego to learn that in addition to the 2,000 coins which were improperly seized, other valuables were missing from his various places of safekeeping. Among them were his mother's 1941 Patek Philippe square, rose-gold watch, $8,000.00 in cash and the first 372 pages of the manuscript of his book. For reasons he never understood, the second 350 pages of the manuscript were left undisturbed. Facing the reality of his desperate situation, he did not raise the issue of the loss to anyone.

While Dr. Aguilar was incarcerated, his wife, Caitlin, hired Sampson & Baumgarten, the lawyers who owned the largest Yellow Page ad in the Lawyers section of the New York phone book. They affected the release of their client from custody, but rather than seek ways to successfully defend the criminal charges against their client, they spent the majority of their time attempting to determine the value of the coins removed from the museum.

They had convinced Dr. Aguilar and the California lawyer he had retained that if the value of the coins exceeded $1,000,000.00 there would be a mandatory five to eight year prison sentence in Sing Sing. It should be noted that the California lawyer was Dr. Aguilar's neighbor, Richard J. Garnett. In an effort to determine the actual value of the coins, Dr. Aguilar, accompanied by his lawyers, Baumgarten, Sampson and Garnett, embarked on a three month journey to Europe in an attempt to valuate the coins.

Eventually, the lawyers engaged in a series of plea-bargain discussions which resulted in an agreement to have Dr. Aguilar plead guilty to a Class D felony which was the lowest level felony in the State of New York. Ultimately, Dr. Aguilar received a six-month jail sentence to be served in San Diego and a $1,000,000.00 fine. This included $160,000.00 in restitution to the ANS Museum to install a new security system and $36,494.92 to cover the costs of the prosecution. The $840,000.00 balance was to be paid to the City of New York as a fine.

Thereafter, Dr. Aguilar began receiving the balance of his coin collection which had been improperly seized. It was then he learned that despite the ANS having been made whole by August 15, 1989, for some unexplained reason, the prosecutor, Rosanne Bertolli, was still delivering coins to the museum as late as November 20, 1990, without regard to the fact that the provenance trail clearly indicated those coins were the property of Dr. Aguilar.

Upon the return of his collection in February of 1991, Dr. Aguilar found that the loss of coins which had not been returned to him exceeded the amount of his required restitution by $250,000.00.

Dr. Aguilar paid the entire amount of restitution of $196,494.92 and the first installment of his fine in the amount of $40,000.00. By 1992, he had run out of money and was unable to pay the next installment. Believing that a violation of probation would send him to Sing Sing prison, he applied for loans with Wells Fargo Bank, but his applications were denied. He listed many of his coins for sale, but was unable to sell them because of the fall of the global markets. For the first time he was frightened by the prospect of going to prison.

To add to his problems, In November, 1992, the California Medical Board chose to take action against his medical license. His situation looked grim.

Then he hired Clyde Munsell.

· ·‖≡●D●C●≡‖· ·

The first thing Clyde observed was that the family was in shambles. As if his legal problems weren't enough, it was discovered that Dr. Aguilar had a mistress. This public disclosure created an impossible situation for Mrs. Aguilar, as a result of which she was determined not to forgive her husband for the embarrassment he brought to the family under any circumstances.

She was so determined, that when Dr. Aguilar hired Clyde Munsell to extricate him from his problems, she intercepted the first two $25,000.00 retainer checks. She destroyed the first one and caused payment to be stopped on the other.

As the December 31, 1992 deadline approached, Dr. Aguilar became so extremely overwrought that his wife believed he would leave the family and flee from the United States to avoid certain imprisonment. However, on December 7, 1992, Dr.

Aguilar was able to deliver a valid check to Clyde Munsell and execute a retainer agreement. The tide began to turn.

Clyde intervened in the family squabble and secured a suspension of the hostilities, to the extent that was possible, so they could direct their energies to the extrication of Dr. Aguilar from the quagmire of his legal entanglements.

He met with Dr. Aguilar's neighbor and local California counsel, Richard Garnett, to discuss his opinions, theories, reasoning and legal analysis of his client's case. Most distressing was his reasoning to justify the $1,000,000.00 fine.

The first thing Clyde did was enter his appearance as substitute counsel in the criminal case. Clyde elected to keep Garnett as counsel in the Medical Board Case to maintain some control over those proceedings and to have him available for consultation if needed.

Clyde learned from an article he read in the New York Times that a number of convictions based upon plea agreements were overturned in New York because of an exclusionary rule involving "sidebars" held in the absence of the accused. Sidebars occur when a discussion between the defendant's lawyer and the prosecutor takes place at the bench out of earshot of the jury. If the defendant is not called to the bench during the sidebar, he too is precluded from hearing what is discussed. The law required that the defendant be present during all phases of his case so he could not only see, but could also hear what was happening.

When Clyde reviewed the record of Dr. Aguilar's hearing on his plea agreement, he learned that there had been at least one sidebar. With the assistance of computer-expert Attorney Harold Lester, a computer search of Lexis Web, a legal research tool on the Internet, they found the citation of the New York case which was the precedent relied upon in the New York cases cited in the Times article.

With that information, Clyde was able to locate the attorney for the defendant in that case. As it turned out, that attorney was a salaried public defender and could not accept outside work. He recommended that Clyde contact Ted Green, an appellate attorney who had recently left the public defender's office to become a partner with Richard Willstatter in White

Plains, New York. After speaking with them, Clyde hired them to serve as local New York counsel for Dr. Aguilar.

By the twenty-third of December, 1992, they were prepared to file the first application to stay the fine. They had to avoid citing Dr. Aguilar's inability to pay the fine as the reason for the stay. The pleadings were filed on the grounds that the imposition of the fine was illegal under the applicable New York law.

They carefully selected December 23rd as the day to present the application because it was believed that the sentencing judge, Malcolm Hunter, was not likely to be available. It was not unusual for high-ranking judges and prosecutors to be unavailable during the Christmas Holidays. In keeping with proper court protocol, that afternoon, they presented themselves in Judge Hunter's department, where the judge's bailiff sent them to Judge Alvin Cole.

Judge Cole was unsuccessful in locating prosecutor Bertolli to summons her to his chambers. At 4:40 p.m., he signed the Order staying the $200,000.00 installment which would have otherwise been due on December 31st. A hearing date was set for January 5, 1993.

Having achieved the first step in what was to become a long trek, they left the courthouse to share the good news with their client. Willstatter and Munsell needed more time to research and refine their argument for a reversal of the imposition of the fine, so they hired Peter Wessel, an independent attorney, to seek an adjournment date. Because Wessel had no information about the case, he could not be questioned as to the intricacies of the pleadings by Judge Hunter, who had retained jurisdiction for all purposes in the case. He performed superbly, obtaining a continuance until late in January.

In their preparation for the next hearing, they noted that attorney Garnett had agreed to the imposition of the high fine because the New York statutes provided for a fine equal to twice the amount of the theft. He failed, however, to read further in the statute which provided that the fine could be levied only to the extent that restitution was not made by the date of sentencing.

By the next court appearance on January 29th, Willstatter and Munsell had developed a theory that the fine could not have been legal under any circumstances. In the Aguilar case, total restitution had been made before the sentencing…double zero is zero! Under the applicable statutes, the maximum fine was only $5,000.00 not $840,000.00. Further research by Willstatter revealed that the restitution of the $160,000.00 plus $36,494.92 paid by Aguilar was illegally imposed since it fell beyond the guidelines for restitution reparations in New York. They prepared pleadings citing both of these theories and supported their position with extensive research.

When this information was presented to the court, Judge Hunter continued the matter until April 13th and directed all counsel to engage in efforts to reach a settlement of the matter. Having prepared for this eventuality, they met with the prosecutor outside of the courtroom. They proposed a settlement which would have abated the balance of the fine and left all of the other conditions unchanged. Bertolli literally laughed at them. Her overwhelming arrogance was just a sample of the attitude she displayed throughout the case.

Completely lacking in candor, tact and courtesy, those effronteries cloaked her ignorance not only of the law, but her lack of understanding, compassion and honesty. Little did they know how matters would turn on her incompetence and dishonesty.

Having been completely rebuffed in their efforts to effect a settlement, Willstatter and Munsell engaged in an intense research program in a determined effort to support a bid to set aside the Aguilar plea agreement. They prepared and filed supplemental pleadings to which they received non-responsive pleadings which were completely off-point, and legally insufficient.

———— ·ːː≡◊●Ɗ◊Ç●≋ːː· ————

Clyde made a decision to take over the medical Board case and dismiss Garnett from further participation. It had become apparent that he was so misinformed and incompetent that he could not be trusted with further management of those proceedings. Likewise, he decided to review the efforts of Sampson & Baumgarten and requested copies of their complete files in the Aguilar matter.

After numerous requests for the files met with no success, he concluded that somebody was hiding something. Clyde went so far as to threaten Sampson & Baumgarten with a complaint to the New York State Bar, and on several occasions sent armed investigators to their offices to retrieve the files. Eventually he obtained a small portion of the files. The vast majority of the files were never recovered. What he did get, had been mismanaged, disorganized and in disarray. Most importantly, the alleged telltale video of Dr. Aguilar's interview with the police was missing.

Munsell and Willstatter had filed demands for additional discovery, but the prosecutor refused to respond. If they wanted to get at the truth, it was clear they would have to conduct their own investigation and start at the beginning.

They learned that Dr. Bishop, who was a recovering alcoholic, was summarily fired within two weeks of Dr. Aguilar's arrest. He fell off the wagon and embarked on a three-year drunk down in the Bowery. They located him behind the locked door of a new Newark, New Jersey museum, employed as the coin curator. When the investigators interviewed him, he was quite friendly and forthcoming until they pushed the wrong button.

He was asked, "Hadn't you agreed that Dr. Aguilar could remove coins for the purpose of photographing them as long as he returned them after the photographs were taken?" Without answering, he exploded and forced the investigators out of the room. He hurriedly made several phone calls, never allowed the discussion to resume and completely dismissed the investigators. This was as good as an admission.

By April first, Munsell and Willstatter had the matter well briefed and were prepared to argue their position if afforded the opportunity on April 13th. However, on April 8th, a decision had already been made. It was delivered in writing on the date scheduled for the hearing. Unbelievably, full concession was won on the fine and the court agreed it could not sentence Dr. Aguilar to any additional time in custody.

Overjoyed with their victory, Willstatter and Munsell set sail on a new course to achieve total victory in what remained of the Aguilar debacle. They had to make a decision as to whether or not they wanted to file for a re-sentencing, which would require a hearing, or merely request a remission of the illegal fine. A hearing would have required Dr. Aguilar to appear for the re-sentencing hearing. However, it had become clear that the Court intended to further invoke its wrath on the lives of Dr. Jose Aguilar and the members of his family. It was a calculated risk.

They had already achieved more than they hoped for and a decision was made to forego the return of the money already paid by Dr. Aguilar, rather than risk the uncertainty of a re-sentencing. The disappearance of the $8,000.00 in cash and his mother's Patek Phillipe gold watch which were improperly seized from his safe when the search warrants were executed was never resolved. After exhaustive investigations and the evidence they produced, the only logical conclusion that could be drawn was that one of the police officers or the prosecutor appropriated the items. There was insufficient evidence to prove it and the cost of continuing the investigations would have exceeded the value of the stolen items.

Dr. Aguilar remained free, his medical license was reinstated and the System devoured its ill-gotten gains.

16
The Private Dick

Drinking is the curse of the litigating class, at least of the class of attorneys Clyde knew in the beginning of his career. Following one particularly bad nightmare where Clyde had been arrested again for assault with a deadly weapon…this time a skate board he borrowed from a boy at a fast food stand, his defense attorney, Jerry, saw fit to hire a licensed private investigator, i.e., *private eye, private detective, private dick* to handle the defense inquiries. His name was Troy…one of the leading PI's in the area.

Troy had been especially well known since the time he had been the defense investigator in the notorious case of Sampson Peck, a black youth who had killed one cop and wounded another, then claimed self-defense; when the authorities' manipulation of evidence was eventually proved, Peck walked free.

Troy's first impression on meeting Clyde was of a fellow suffering from alcoholic semi-paralysis, who had to lift up on his left trouser leg to help himself step up or down at a curb. Luckily this was toward the end of Clyde's drinking escapades. Following a successful result in the assault with a deadly weapon case, Troy and Clyde became friendly.

As Clyde began his rise to prominence as a criminal defense lawyer, he used Troy's services regularly. This included a variety of cases in many other states. Over the years, Clyde was never aware and could never have guessed that Troy was homosexual, a fact carefully hidden by the private dick and his live-in associates.

As a community service, Troy had established a day care facility for adolescent boys from troubled homes. What should have been a tip-off, when visiting Troy's office, was his collection of pin-up photos of lads in red swimming briefs. However, in those pre-gay liberation days, the red trunks were something which non-insiders might easily have assumed to be a youth sports club uniform. It never occurred to any outsider that Troy might be *different* since he and his friends did not seem peculiar, and they certainly never discussed their unusual interests. Way back then, it wasn't only don't ask, don't tell...nobody who didn't have to even thought about such things.

Eventually, some of the boys began complaining to their foster or real parents that something was amiss at Troy's day care center. Finally one parent brought the matter to the Office of the District Attorney. The Assistant D.A. assigned to investigate and bring charges was in a frenzy to proceed, due to the infamy of the accusations and because Troy was hated by local law-enforcement since the Peck case. In his eagerness, the A.D.A. did not wait to confer with the leading prosecutor at the time, who happened to have been on vacation.

Harvey Barron, who later became a judge, was a consummate professional and every defense lawyer's nightmare. As a result, the police acted prematurely in executing a search warrant and making an arrest based solely on the complaint of the boy, without wiring him up to get a tape recording that would have firmly nailed Troy. Troy and his two live-in associates were all charged with heinous crimes carrying maximum prison sentences of 268 consecutive years each. This was front-page news, of course.

Clyde arranged for the hiring of two *speak-easies*, puppet lawyers who would do as Clyde directed, to represent Troy's pair of companion defendants. The case began in earnest when Harvey got back from vacation and learned Clyde was involved. Harvey and Clyde had been fast friends since Clyde successfully represented Harvey's father in a multi-million-dollar international fraud case out of Florida and Detroit. Harvey warned Clyde to butt-out of Troy's defense.

However, Clyde thought despicable cases needed serious defenses to protect the adversarial system of justice from being corrupted as a result of negligent representation. Besides, the defendant had also been a longtime, loyal and reliable expert and associate who had unfailingly been of service to Clyde and his clients.

Clyde's first move was to maneuver the case into the courtroom of Judge Fred Frank. Clyde had been in the same class at law school with this jurist, and knew him to be cosmopolitan and emancipated enough not to let prejudicial, knee-jerk, conventional sexual attitudes interfere with the workings of the law. Unless presented by indictment, all criminal cases at that time began in Municipal Court to stand the test of a preliminary hearing before being bound over for trial in Superior Court. Most cases were not vertically integrated, so a new prosecutor had to pick it up and get reorganized at every level of the proceedings. However, the Office of the District Attorney had begun to change that procedure in some specialized areas including child molestation so the prosecutor who began the case could take it through to its conclusion

Since the D.A.'s office already had some problems with Troy's case due to the premature arrest before the evidentiary hook was set by getting a self-inculpating tape-recording of the defendants, Harvey decided to handle the prosecution personally. This was a problem for Clyde, because Harvey was inevitably dauntless, effective, and extremely well prepared. He was the best the D.A. had at the time...one of the best ever... and all but unbeatable. Harvey was a humane gentleman to the utmost, but gave no quarter in courtroom confrontations. He was nobody's fool, and he wasn't fooling around.

In those days the penal code was organized into several classes: misdemeanors; felonies which could be adjudged misdemeanors, referred to as wobblers; and straight felonies...punishable only by prison sentences unless probation was granted. Harvey told Clyde he would agree to an eight year prison sentence across the board if Troy pled to a felony so the case would not go to a preliminary hearing and the young boy would not need to testify.

Child molesters never fare well in the prison system. They are offenders whom the violent felons, who occupy a superior position in the hierarchy of the convict population, attack and abuse devoutly, without consequences. Nowadays, prison authorities keep molesters in protective separation, which amounts to solitary confinement, to keep fatality statistics down. In the time of Troy's case, security for such endangered inmates was nonchalant and a lot of molesters didn't survive. So any prison term was a possible death sentence. Clyde couldn't risk that deal, and began seeking a safe evacuation route for his client.

Clyde filed a demurrer challenging the sufficiency of the complaint. Because this procedure is rarely used in criminal courts, it is particularly effective in distracting the prosecution, since the D.A.'s office is not practiced at handling it. The mere filing of the demurrer precludes the entry of any plea, guilty or not guilty, and stops the process in its tracks. Minimally, the defense can obtain vast quantities of useful information as they dig through the strata of the case on the D.A.'s time, poking ever deeper to find whatever can be found.

In Troy's case, the D.A. was able to show the complaint was properly drawn, but in the discovery of the information leading up to that point some gems were found that Clyde and his puppet crew could use for cutting into and grinding up the prosecution's weapons.

Next, Clyde filed a traversal motion to quash the search warrant in front of the same judge who had signed it, which forced the judge to re-examine and second-guess his previous position. If he could be persuaded that he was deceived or mistaken in any way, he might reverse his decision on the search warrant. This motion causes the prosecutors to disclose evidence before the preliminary examination which they might otherwise have hidden until getting into the Superior Court trial process. In this case, it disclosed a mother-lode jackpot for the defense.

As it turned out, in the affidavits for the search warrant the judge had been told that one of Troy's co-defendant associates had photographed the young boys repeatedly in various degrees of undress, including total nudity, and that the boy who was the complainant was one of those photographed naked. Clyde subpoenaed all the photos the prosecution had. At the hearing, it became picture-clear to the judge that no such photos existed and that the officers swearing out the search warrant had perjured themselves, apparently expecting the evidence they would find would support the guesses they had sworn to as facts. Clyde further pounded the nail by entertainingly questioning the evidentiary value of one of the seized photos, which was of Elvis Presley in concert. So the search warrant was quashed, eliminating all the physical evidence seized as *fruit of the poisonous tree*. Thus, the prosecution had to proceed only on the boy's proposed testimony with no other supporting evidence.

Clyde's next move was to get a court order for Judge Frank to retain jurisdiction for all purposes, meaning he would hear the preliminary examination and the plea and anything else so long as the case remained in Municipal Court. Keeping Judge Frank was vital...nowhere *upstairs* in Superior Court would Clyde find a jurist as broad-minded and already ticked-off at the prosecution by the search warrant fiasco.

After obtaining releases of all the defendants, Clyde put the preliminary exam on continuance and began earnestly negotiating a plea arrangement, confident the prosecution would want to avoid having the young victim testify and be cross-examined publicly, in the presence of the news media. Those were the days after the era of closed preliminary examinations., and before officers were allowed to testify on behalf of minors.

About this time, the defense got an unintended boost from an unexpected source...Clyde's ex-wife, who was vindictively and constantly trying to do him dirt. Of course, it was in the public interest and as a concerned mother (HA!) that she complained to the Office of the District Attorney that her children and all others in the community were at risk because the defendants might get light treatment due to Clyde having once successfully defended the prosecutor's father. Very properly, Harvey immediately withdrew, from the case and refused any further participation in the prosecution effort. Since he was the best district attorney in the office, this irreparably damaged the prosecution's effectiveness and greatly advanced the position of Clyde's defense...a scorching backfire in the face of the malicious ex-wife.

The D.A.'s office had only one openly homosexual prosecutor, who had founded a gay lawyer's rights organization. Being an avowed member of the same fraternity as the defendants and also being well known as an inept lawyer, he was the worst possible choice to lead the prosecution. Yet, in a classic example of bureaucratic boondoggling, he was the one appointed to take over the case. He could get no help from Harvey, who had recused himself and, not unnaturally, he got no help from anyone else in the department.

There were many complex nuances in the laws governing the case, and many more in the Clyde Code of defense maneuvers. Asking this particular attorney to prosecute the case was like asking an eye surgeon to operate in the dark.

Clyde proceeded to inundate him with subpoena upon subpoena and motion upon motion. Soon, all could see symptoms of drowning desperation in the prosecutor's haggard expression and raddled eyeballs. Everyone could see he was not going to stay afloat in this case for long.

Then Clyde filed a motion for a civil compromise, which was allowed in some misdemeanor matters, even over the objection of the District Attorney, if the victim would accept restitution for complete redress in the case...in other words, how much it would take to get the complainant to not testify. If such a motion were granted by the Municipal Court judge, the case would be dismissed even if the D.A. objected.

The section allowing civil compromise does not apply to all misdemeanors; for instance, it would not apply to a drunk driving case. An identifiable victim is necessary, not merely The People of The State of California. Troy's case had an individual identifiable as a victim, but the sexual abuse charges were felonies, and therefore not subject to civil compromise unless the judge first decided they were misdemeanors. In some of those cases, that was possible with some of the charges, though in most instances it was not.

Clyde filed the motion on the grounds that the vague and ambiguous area of child molestation charges throughout the

California criminal code was such that it was up to the judge, not the defense, to determine which was and was not eligible for civil compromise. It was also up to the victim if the rather hefty sum offered was acceptable. Clyde offered his entire fee, a strong five-figure sum, figuring if they took this and the case was dismissed, everybody could go home happy.

The victim, through his parents, did not accept the sum. Clyde was not surprised they could not be bought off. The case went forward. Moreover, the judge indicated he would not allow a civil compromise anyway since even though he had offered a rubber stamp for his name on all of Clyde's motions and orders in the case, he would not allow a civil compromise in a child molestation case. Frankly, that was the right thing for him to do, but Clyde learned a great deal more about the case, much to the disadvantage of the District Attorney. While the victim was willing to testify, his testimony turned out to be much weaker than had originally appeared. There was an extreme probability the D.A. would be unable to prove the case at trial.

At this juncture Clyde turned up the heat. He explained his plan to the puppet lawyers. Between the three of them they rubbed eyeballs, followed, cajoled, and badgered the prosecutor each and every hour of his day. There was never a time he could concentrate on any other case, since he was always looking in the faces of Clyde and his two colleagues.

Clyde also held daily meetings with the entire defense crew, each member reporting the results of what they discovered and the feelings they had developed about the case. Clyde really didn't give a damn what the other defense lawyers felt; they were accustomed to losing...Clyde never lost. He knew it was the time to strike. He scheduled a meeting late on a Friday morning before a three day weekend at the prosecutor's office. The purpose of the meeting was announced in advance...was there a plea available, and if so, what would it be? The prosecutor normally would go to his superiors seeking guidance and establishing the parameters of the deal. In this instance, his superiors and even his confederates would not talk to him about the case...he was marooned on a sinking island, way over his head in a case of this complexity and notoriety.

Knowing the prosecutor would be anxious to eat, Clyde,

powering on a late breakfast, argued for two and one-half hours, right through lunchtime...until 1:30 in the afternoon. By that time, the prosecutor was out of energy. He agreed to local time commitments for all three defendants. In the California system, local time meant incarceration in a county jail, with no possibility of State prison, no matter what the defendants did. So, they would not face the very real prospect of getting murdered in prison.

This was a time to rejoice. Not letting any grass grow under his feet, Clyde took the matter that very afternoon to Judge Frank for an impromptu conference. He knew that although the judge left early on Fridays, he stuck around long enough so he wouldn't be missed. Clyde got to him by 2:30 p.m., with the prosecutor in tow, negotiating with the judge to nail down the proposed sentences for the defendants.

To give the case propriety and make it appear the D.A. was fighting hard, Clyde offered three different counts, one for each of the defendants, such that the press would not see it as a roll-over or a packaged deal which, of course, was exactly what it was. But, the public never understands what's going on behind the scenes anyway. What Clyde was attempting to do was to save three lives by avoiding the dangers of prison...so far, so good.

At first, Judge Frank offered an attractive deal...no time for Troy's co-defendant on his misdemeanor, six months for his other co-defendant on the wobbler, and one year local time for Troy. Clyde liked the deal and took it to the clients. Being the most at risk, Troy told his buddies to take the deal and he would take the weight.

The next court day, Clyde was back in Judge Frank's department, pushing to finalize the deal before anything cooled off. By that time, the judge realized the heat he would take for what he was doing...he'd never be re-elected if the defendants got off this easy. He had to make the deal stronger. He wanted two years for Troy, back-to-back local time, but keep the deal on the two co-defendants. Clyde knew Troy would take this to make sure his friends got easy deals. One of his friends faced only twelve days in jail, which he never served since the County Jail didn't accept prisoners for less than 30 days.

Although Troy's other friend pled to a felony with a six-month sentence, it was to be reduced to a misdemeanor upon successful completion of probation, so Clyde was able to get him sentenced to work furlough. Clyde knew the work furlough program would not take a sex offender, so when that couldn't be accomplished, Clyde asked for house arrest. That was considered to be too light, so it was settled he'd actually serve only 30 days in County Jail on the six-month sentence.

Troy began to serve his sentence. A year on top of a year meant he would be out in about fourteen months. He had to do this in County Jail, since no camp or work furlough program would take him, and house arrest was out of the question. By that time, Clyde's win record in felony pursuits against the D.A. was well over 2,500 and closer to 3,000. Moreover, because Troy's despicable crime had been committed over a long period of time, affected over 200 boys, and because he had once contributed to acquittal of a cop-killer, he was even more unpopular within The System than Clyde.

The politicians, bureaucrats, prosecutors, and law enforcement personnel who worked for The System were quite willing to manipulate the rules to seek revenge on those who prevailed against it. The *Enemies of The System* were invisibly marked, as effectively as being branded with a scarlet letter or garbed with a yellow star, never to be forgotten or forgiven.

So Troy was a marked man. He was also diabetic, requiring an insulin injection every day. However, diabetics going to jail are not allowed to take their insulin with them. The jail is supposed to administer needed medications and prescription drugs under court order. But the jail personnel of The System were not about to care for Troy's health which resulted in *clerical errors*. When the jail personnel read the court order for Troy's insulin, they administered aspirin. When they read the order for blood thinners, they gave him a topical solution like lanolin.

Clyde, who was visiting Troy daily at that time, told him to keep a written journal of all the wrongs being committed against him. Clyde started filing motions and dragging the jail hospital staff into Judge Frank's department. The hospital staff routinely said they were giving him all the necessary health treatment he was supposed to be getting. After ninety days, Troy's health was so bad Clyde got court orders for other doctors to examine Troy in jail and examine his medical records. They reported to Judge

Frank that the whole situation was deplorable. The System was implacable and impervious to the orders of the court and the treatment recommended by the doctors.

Clyde and Troy realized they were being baited for Clyde to attempt smuggling Troy's medications into jail, so The System could fall on Clyde as well. Clyde and Troy agreed not to fall for that, although Troy's health continued to worsen. Clyde took Troy's journal notes and filed a motion to terminate Troy's custody because he was not being given proper medical attention and his life was in jeopardy. The motion was heard on a Friday morning. Having set the stage so well, even though fourteen members of the jail personnel, including the chief doctor all testified Troy was receiving proper treatment, the four-hour hearing showed Judge Frank their testimony was not credible... actually it was perjurious.

Troy was released forthwith and the following Monday reported to a private work furlough Clyde had arranged and which the court accepted for Troy to serve out his sentence while getting real medical care. Troy spent Monday in the work furlough, got sick that night and died Tuesday morning.

Though Troy was not guilty of a capital crime under the law, The System had succeeded in executing him for crimes against it...death by fatal systematic disregard of The System's legal obligation to provide inmate medical care. Clyde reported this to Judge Frank the same day Troy died. Of course, they both knew The System could not be prosecuted for assassination.

Clyde wrote a 492-page letter to the U.S. Department of Justice detailing the jail's complicity in Troy's wrongful death. Troy's situation was only one in the jail's long history of human rights abuses. A Federal investigation ensued unlike any to which the jail had ever been subjected. The institution was not reformed, of course, though it was thoroughly agitated and had to become more defensively devious. Any conspicuous enemy of The System is among an endangered species. Troy's death at the hands of the system was a clear message. This was when Clyde decided to escape from his long, successful criminal defense career and limit his practice to tax law, where he continues to apply his winning strategies.

17
Epilogue

There are a number of terms used to describe criminal defense lawyers...none of them particularly complimentary. *Mouthpiece, pettifogger, ganef* and *shyster* are a few of the more popular ones among the other more obscene terms.

The common and popular view of defense lawyers to a great extent arises from the misperceptions of the public generated by the entertainment industry. It has a long history of portraying lawyers like Perry Mason, whose clients are always acquitted because he solves the crime during the course of the trial, or programs which adversely portray lawyers who are sleaze bags attempting to divert attention from their guilty client to some innocent party.

As against such idealized fantasies, a large faction of cynics are temperamentally convinced that defense lawyers are the driving force of a criminal justice system that is coddling criminals and creating an epidemic of human predators.

The general image of lawyers is further tarnished by the bias of the mainstream media which never misses an opportunity to paint lawyers as miscreants and sully the reputation of all lawyers because of the misdeeds of a few. Rarely, if ever, do you read about the positive achievements of the legal profession and its contributions to a civil and just society. Good news doesn't sell newspapers or attract a television audience.

In actual practice, defense lawyers are just field hands laboring to cultivate justice. Not the romantic impartial justice depicted by the marble statue of a blindfolded goddess with a sword in one hand and the divinely balanced scales in the other; nor the theoretical and philosophical abstraction of ivory tower Justice with a capital "J." The criminal defense attorney is engaged in the begriming work of producing fruit from the manure of crime and punishment that can nourish, rather than poison a nation conceived in liberty.

It is the justice of keeping the prosecutorial power machine of a monolithic government fair and honest. It is the relentless task of requiring functional compliance with historic principles of due process. It is an effort to eke out of chaos a tempering mercy to provide hope for an opportunity to be rehabilitated instead of being abandoned to self-perpetuating recidivism. In short, it is using the adversarial system of jurisprudence to actually benefit people, rather than letting it default into the pure inquisitorial despotism of a police state.

Under our system of jurisprudence, it is the duty and obligation of a defense lawyer to do everything possible, within the scope of the law, to defend his client and free him from the yoke of prosecution. In doing so, the lawyer is forbidden to take his client's guilt or innocence into consideration. This concept is expressly established in the professional canons of ethics of the organized Bar and is incorporated in the laws which every attorney has taken a solemn oath to uphold. It is the essential structural support of a long-acknowledged tenet of justice in our culture: *"It is better that ten guilty persons go free than one innocent person suffer."*...William Blackstone, Commentaries on the Laws of England, 1765.

Acknowledgements

First and foremost, my sincere thanks to my friend, Ron Sharrow, Attorney, and author of the Bruce West Novels who generously edited and gave time and effort to help publish this book. Without his encouragement, suggestions, writing skills and knowledge of self-publishing, these stories would still be stored away in a filing cabinet.

My gratitude to my long time friend, Loring G. Fillebrown, who transcribed and re-wrote my notes about each story. His association with me and my office over the last half-century were invaluable.

Without God's help to find my way from the depths of depravity through a Twelve Step Program, I would never have achieved the successes I enjoyed in my 40 plus years of the practice of law. With His help, I discovered the rewards of helping countless others to achieve sobriety.

Thou sparkling bowl...thou sparkling bowl!
Though lips of bards thy brim may press,
And eyes of beauty o'er thee roll,
And song and dance thy power confess,
I will not touch thee; for there clings
A scorpion to thy side, that stings.
~ John Pierpont, 1879.

About the Author

Clyde Munsell earned a BS degree in accounting from San Diego State College in 1967 and his JD degree from California Western School of Law in 1971. After passing the California State Bar Examination on his first application in 1971, he was admitted to the practice of law in California in January, 1972.

With his accounting degree and prior accounting experience in two National CPA firms, he established his private law practice emphasizing taxation and criminal defense. He is admitted to practice before the United States Tax Court.

Clyde has successfully defended clients in major criminal and tax cases in numerous jurisdictions; among them, Arizona, California, Florida, Illinois, Kansas, Louisiana, Michigan, Montana, Nevada, New Mexico, New York, Tennessee, Texas and Wyoming. He has also handled cases in Canada, Mexico and Sweden.

Praise for Loophole

"Lessons on how to succeed as a criminal defense attorney: find a flaw...abrade it...chafe it...irritate it...gnaw on it and inflame it until it explodes and destroys your adversary."
~ Richard W. Hanawalt, Attorney

"Great examples of how to manipulate the criminal justice system to achieve jaw-dropping results without going to trial."
~ Samuel Arthur Sue III, Attorney

"How a criminal defense lawyer achieved successful results simply by forcing the government to cross its T's, dot its I's and follow its own rules."
~ James A. Watson, CPA

"Non-fiction accounts of criminal cases that read like novels. A must read for law students, practicing lawyers and everyone with an abiding trust in the United States Constitution"
~ David Bryant, Director - Rancho Mirage Public Library